# Reaching for the Stars

# Reaching for the Stars

*The Entertainers Prayerbook*

Chris Gidney

CANTERBURY
PRESS
Norwich

© Chris Gidney 2009

First published in 2009 by the Canterbury Press Norwich
Editorial office
13–17 Long Lane,
London, EC1A 9PN, UK

Canterbury Press is an imprint of Hymns Ancient and
Modern Ltd (a registered charity)
St Mary's Works, St Mary's Plain,
Norwich, NR3 3BH, UK

www.scm-canterburypress.co.uk

British Library Cataloguing in Publication data
A catalogue record for this book is available
from the British Library

978-1-85311-970-5

Typesetting by Regent Typesetting, London
Printed and bound in Great Britain by
CPI Bookmarque, Croydon, Surrey

# Contents

# CONTENTS

# CONTENTS

# Curtain Up

It was one of my most embarrassing moments. I didn't know the couple who had invited me to lunch that well, so I was determined to be on my best behaviour. I turned up on their doorstep with the usual bunch of flowers and chocolates and was soon ushered to a white table beautifully laid. My taste buds anticipated the appetizer that started to arrive – until I saw what was on mine. Salami. Yuk. I hated salami. As I stared down at a whole plate of the stuff I went into panic mode. I decided to resort to the only thing I could think of: the art of sleight of hand. It was something that at that moment I was very grateful to my magician father for teaching me many years before.

Still keeping a friendly smile towards the other guests but quicker than the eye could see, I managed to pretend I was eating the meat while slowly palming the slices down from my plate and on to my lap. I was greatly relieved to see that none of the other diners had a clue as to what was happening. I thought all was well.

The problem came when into the room amid the jollity of the occasion marched a fit-looking dog. It stared around for a while and then dived straight under the table. I could feel it brush up against my trousers before it suddenly grabbed a slice of meat from my lap and started to chew it noisily on the floor beneath us. It must have been my controlled jump as the dog knocked against my legs that made my host look at me and then peer under the table. Fortunately, the dog had finished the meaty morsel by then and I had the presence of mind to cover the remains of the meat on my lap with a serviette. The dog was banned from the room. All was still well.

The rest of the lunch party went smoothly and I was relieved to know that my little secret was now secure. The one problem I had was when the time came to get up from my seat to relax on the sofa with a coffee. It was no problem really as by that time I had stuffed the poor old bits of rejected salami into my trouser pocket.

We all rose like a courtroom, but in came that blasted dog again. It bounded straight up to me so fast that it nearly knocked me over. Then to my horror it began licking the lap of my trousers and barking wildly. The owner looked at me strangely again and shouted at the dog. The dog was having none of it, and the other guests watched aghast at the leaping, pushing and whining that followed me wherever I tried to escape. I eventually sat down again, but it jumped straight on top of me sniffing and pawing at me in a most uncomfortable and embarrassing place while I struggled to push it off.

The owner was too shocked to know what to do, so I knew I just had to get rid of the salami somehow and as quickly as possible. My hosts were speechless as to why their normally quiet pet was determined to give me such unwarranted attention. I could feel their strong gaze penetrating my back as I quickly left to go to the toilet – closely followed by their dog. It was difficult enough trying to get into the bathroom without the dog joining me, but eventually I pushed it away and eased the door shut. At last, alone and breathless, I unpacked every last bit of salami from my pocket and dropped it into the toilet. I pulled the chain, but to my dismay saw that the meat would not flush down the pan. I tried several times, but for some reason it just would not go down. I tried everything, and what the guests imagined was going on while hearing continual flushing, I couldn't bring myself to consider.

With the dog still barking at the door, I left the bathroom, relieved that it would now leave me alone. Within seconds of sitting back on the sofa the dog had leapt on me again, with even more fervour than before. My heart sank when I realized that the fragrance of the meat must have gone deeper than I thought into my trousers and the dog was now more frantic than ever. There was only one solution: I had to leave. With a very red face, I explained that I had to suddenly get back home and the shocked and bewildered look on the faces of everyone in the room is something I shall never forget.

Walking away, I wondered what they would think when they saw bits of meat floating about in their loo. The trousers got thrown away, I am now very wary of dogs, I hate salami more than ever and, funnily enough, I never got invited back.

You would have thought I had learned my lesson, but three weeks later I was invited to another lunch party, this time at the home of a French foot juggler, Jean Claude, and Yvette, his wife. I sat at the table only to be offered a shellfish starter beautifully placed within a clamshell. I can't eat fish, and I started to gag. I just couldn't help myself. This time, though, the thought of a creamy sauce in my trouser pocket didn't seem like an option so I used the retching of my system as cover to down the dish almost in one go. I was greatly relieved. Yvette was so bemused at how fast I had eaten her pièce de résistance that she immediately left for the kitchen and brought me another. I nearly choked to death as I went through the whole procedure all over again.

They say that 'honesty is the best policy' and I think that from these experiences that's certainly right. If only I had had the guts to say I didn't like, or couldn't eat, the food being offered to me. I was risking upsetting my hosts, but perhaps that would not have been as bad as I might have imagined. The one that we don't upset by being honest with is God. It's so refreshing to know that he loves us and accepts us just as we are. Someone once wrote, 'God is never disillusioned with us because he never has illusions about us in the first place'.

When I talk to my heavenly Father I can be totally honest about how I feel or what I have done, or how my thinking is, and still be assured that he will never think badly of me. He will understand, encourage and guide. He's the best Dad there is.

However, praying can be difficult at the best of times, and sometimes incredibly boring for us – and perhaps God too! Here, in these pages, actors from Doctor Who to Poirot, performers from *The Phantom of the Opera* to *The Lion King*, and comedians from Tim Vine to Ken Dodd, offer the prayers they have enjoyed or written for their own use – whether they were on top of the world or down in the dumps.

The host of performers included here from all areas of the entertainment industry will appeal to those of every age, background and spiritual experience.

The prayers my showbiz friends have sent me vary from hilarious to sad, to reflective and thought-provoking. Some are honest enough to suggest they have doubts or are still searching for answers. Some, like the Escapologist's Prayer, may seem irrelevant until one realizes that we all have things that can tie us up and trap us, and that this prayer asks for freedom for us all. I have found these different prayers all helpful in their own way, coming from those whose very profession it is to effectively communicate to an audience.

Interestingly, many celebrities have worries and fears just like the rest of us. For example, I've heard that Johnny Depp has clourophobia, a fear of clowns; Nicole Kidman has mottephobia, a fear of butterflies; Cheryl Cole has bambakomallophobia, a fear of cotton wool; and David Beckham has ataxophobia, a fear of untidiness!

The good news is that we have access to one of the world's best ways of achieving tranquillity in our lives, and I hope that the prayers, stories and behind-the-scenes glimpses of performers' lives will inspire and enthuse you to do what Doddy calls 'keeping in touch with the boss upstairs'.

So in your prayers be honest with God today. He's the most trustworthy and dependable friend there is.

Chris Gidney
*April 2009*

# John Archer

John Archer has been voted the Magic Circle Stage Magician of the Year and has spent 20 years entertaining audiences all over the world with his expertise, comedy and sleight of hand. But is it OK to be a Christian and a magician?

John explains, 'When the Bible uses the terms "magic" or "sorcery", it is clearly dealing with an involvement in the supernatural, and makes it clear that God does not want us to dabble in such perilous games. Today's manifestations of these forbidden activities are such things as ouija boards, tarot cards and the occult. The Christian has no business playing with these, since they open the door to influences that are often dangerous. Let it be emphasized that no true Christian magician is in any way involved in the use of supernatural powers; instead, it is pure trickery and so offers a fun and visual way of demonstrating the gospel. It is a highly respected art form and there is even an Association of Christian Magicians which uses the wonderful visuality of the illusionist to talk about spiritual matters.'

As a highly respected member of the entertainment business, John was recently awarded The Ken Dodd Presidents Trophy for Best New Magical Comedy Entertainer. When John took part in the British Magical Championships, he was awarded British Magical Champion of Comedy and then promoted to Member of the Inner Magic Circle – and awarded the Carlton Comedy Award for outstanding use of comedy and magic.

As someone who does not seek to hide his faith, John believes that Christians in all walks of life should strive to do their very best with the talents God has invested in them. Television magician and psychological illusionist Derren Brown says, 'Booking an act for my dad's 70th birthday, I wanted a great act and went straight to John Archer. His reputation in the magic world is among the very best. I was so pleased he was able to do it, and he absolutely brought the house down. It was brilliant, hysterically funny, and perfectly pitched for the occasion. He made the evening. I'd recommend him unreservedly.'

Although John Archer spends a lot of time in the secular world of entertainment, his strong Christian faith means that much of his remaining time is spent doing church-based work. John has worked at many of the big festivals, including Spring Harvest, New Wine, Soul Survivor, Cross-fire, Greenbelt and Roots. He enjoys the opportunity to perform at thousands of regular and irregular church events of all types, including pub, hotel or club events, street work, youth work, family services, seminars on creativity, and comedy writing every year which he considers essential for Bible students.

Sometimes he dares to offer Christians pure entertainment. 'After all,' he says, 'it's not a sin. I've checked!'

John has written his own prayer, which is one we can all pray no matter what job we are involved in.

## The Magician's Prayer

Father God, please bless these trivial things I do tonight that they might glorify your name.

Help me to show that you have so much more up your sleeve than I could ever have. Cause the people to be gently taken from illusion to reality and let my mysteries clearly point people to seek the answer to the biggest mystery of life itself.

May your presence and love be found in every joke and magical moment, and may the words that I speak reach the hearts of your people and cause them to draw closer to you.

May the talent that you have given me, be given back to you tonight well used.

But most of all, Lord, I pray that the greatest trick they see tonight is that I vanish and you appear. Amen.

## Cannon & Ball

Cannon & Ball have been hailed as Britain's own Kings of Comedy, and it's easy to see why. In a career spanning more than 35 years, they have achieved a string of honours that puts them among the 'greats' of showbusiness.

From 11 years of their own television series to starring in several Royal Variety Performances, they have become one of the best-known television comedy acts. Their ability to consistently sell out in all the major theatre venues has made them the kings of live entertainment, and their pantomime run at the world-famous London Palladium broke all box office records when it took the largest amount ever taken in one week in British theatre history. They are still as busy as ever.

Nor have they been free from all the difficulties of being in the public eye. The newspapers often try to dig up some sort of story from the past, sometimes even trying to disprove their Christian faith. But as Bobby says, 'The career is not as important as our relationship with God. He pulled me out of a pit and set my feet on a rock, and I'll love him for ever for that.'

**Bobby Ball** loves writing his own poems, and his chosen prayer is the closing section of one poem he has written.

## Power of Praise

Please forgive me, but I find it hard to apologize,
To be able to see the other person's point of view.
But deep inside, behind all this sinful pride,
I want to be just like you.

Really deep in my soul, I want to be sensitive,
I want to open my eyes and see.
I no longer want this pride to be ever consuming,
I want to trade for humility.

As Jesus said, pride is a sin
And it will eventually bring about a man's fall.
You see, I've been too busy being proud
I didn't listen to Jesus' call.

If only you could forgive me, Jesus,
For my sins, but most of all my pride.
Forgive, for all the people my pride hurt,
And for the way to myself I lied.

So fill me, Jesus, with your love,
Fill me to my innermost being.
Take away this mask from my eyes,
Give me joy like a blind man first upon seeing.

Earnestly I beg you, Jesus,
Wash away my sin as only you can,
And turn this arrogant and ignorant thing
Into a brand new humble man.

**Tommy Cannon** says prayer can be pretty confusing: 'If God knows everything, why do we need to pray at all? I think I found part of the answer recently when I suddenly got a text from my grandson. I hadn't seen him for a while, but I'd not forgotten him. When his text came through it brought him nearer to my mind and I sent a text back and started a conversation. Perhaps that's what prayer is like? When, amid our busy lives, we decide to send God a quick prayer, we know he already cares about us, but this allows him to enter our lives again. Here's a prayer that reminds me how fickle we are and it makes me laugh every time I read it.'

## The Dieter's Prayer

Lord, my soul is ripped with riot,
Incited by my wicked diet.

'We are what we eat,' said a wise old man.
Lord, if that's true, I'm a garbage can.

I want to rise on Judgment Day, that's plain,
But at my present weight I'll need a crane.

So grant me strength that I may not fall
Into the clutches of cholesterol.

May my flesh with carrot curls be sated,
That my soul may be polyunsaturated.

And show me the light that I may bear witness
To the Government's Council on Physical Fitness.

Give me this day, my daily slice
But cut it thin and toast it twice.

I beg upon my dimpled knees,
Deliver me from those Smarties.

I can do it, Lord, if you'll show to me
The virtues of lettuce and celery.

And when my days of trial are done
And my war with malted milk is won,

Let me stand with the saints in heaven
In a shining robe, size 37!

Author unknown

## A Little Boy's Prayer

Dear God, please take care of my daddy,
mummy, sister, brother, my doggy and me.
Oh yes, and please take care of yourself, God.
If anything happens to you, we're gonna be in a big
mess.

# Julian Battersby

Julian Battersby has appeared in numerous films and in the
West End, including the most famous and longest running
hit of all, *The Mousetrap*. 'I have heard various ministers remind me that the Greek word for actor is hypocrite,' Julian
says. 'This is my actor's prayer, and one that I think can be
used in everyday life.'

## Hypocrite's Prayer

Dear heavenly Father,
Please touch me with your artistry and help me to give a
good performance, without being a hypocrite. Amen.

A few days before Christmas, two young brothers were
spending the night at their grandparents' house. When it
was time to go to bed, and anxious to do the right thing,
they both knelt down to say their prayers.

Suddenly, the younger one began to do so in a very
loud voice. 'Dear Lord, please ask Santa Claus to bring
me a PlayStation, a mountain-bike and a telescope.'

His older brother leaned over and nudged his brother
and said, 'Why are you shouting your prayers? God isn't
deaf.'

'I know,' he replied. 'But Grandma is!'

# Russell Boulter

Russell Boulter is best known as D. S. Boulton in the popular hit television series *The Bill*. Russell actually began
his career with the Royal Shakespeare Company in 1985.
Having the unique ability to play characters right across
the spectrum of classic, musical, comedy and television,
Russell's professional theatre credits range from *Hamlet* at
the Bristol Old Vic to *Blood Brothers* in London's West End.
On television he has been in a whole range of programmes,
from *The Darling Buds of May* to *Casualty*.

When contracted to a television company there is a lot of pressure to learn lines extremely quickly, and when not 'on camera' you will notice Russell in a corner somewhere going through the day's script. You can be called to work at any time of day or night, and this plays havoc with Russell's personal and social life, not to mention church life!

When asked if he feels whether acting is an appropriate career for a Christian, Russell says, 'I think the question for the previous generation of Christians who wanted to pursue an acting career was, "Dare I use this talent for God?" The question for my generation is "Dare I NOT use this talent for God?"

'The Jesus I met in the Gospels was radically different from the Jesus I had been told about in school RE classes. This Jesus was dangerous and exciting. He turned over the money changers' tables, called religious hypocrites "sons of snakes", and healed the broken-hearted. He was accused of being a drunkard at wedding parties, of hanging out with prostitutes and lepers, he cast out devils, he had authority, he was brave, fearsome and passionate, and I really liked him!'

### Visionary's Prayer

Riches I need not, nor all the world's praise,
thou mine inheritance through all my days;
thou, and thou only, the first in my heart,
high King of heaven, my treasure thou art!

Author unknown, Irish (c. eighth century), trans. Mary Byrne,
(1880–1931) and Eleanor Hull (1860–1935)

Russell adds, 'Be thou *my* vision, O Lord I pray.'

'Give us this day our daily bread, and forget not our emails.'

## Faith Brown

Faith Brown is an actor, comedienne and impressionist, noted for her versatility. She began her career as a singer at the age of 15 and her television career was launched with appearances on *Who Do You Do?*, a showcase for a generation of impressionists and comics, and *Ken Dodd's World of Laughter*.

She famously used split screen special effects, and interviewed herself in a succession of celebrity personas including Pam Ayres, Barbra Streisand, Lene Lovich, Angela Rippon, Eartha Kitt, Diana Ross, Mary Whitehouse, and Donna Summer. She has also appeared as Anne Bradley in the television series *Brookside*, and as Flast in the *Doctor Who* episode called 'Attack of the Cybermen'.

Faith starred to great acclaim as faded screen icon Norma Desmond in the UK touring production of the Andrew Lloyd Webber musical *Sunset Boulevard*, releasing a CD of songs from the show. In November 2006, she appeared as a contestant in the sixth series of *I'm a Celebrity Get Me Out Of Here* and became the third celebrity to be voted off the show having spent 14 days in the jungle.

'When I get to heaven I'm going to ask God why he created man first, and why us women have so much more to cope with than the guys,' Faith says. 'At the end of the day I know that he cares about us girls and loves us, but I still pray . . .'

## Why Create Man, God?

Dear God,
Why does . . . Woman have Man in it?
Mrs has Mr in it?
Female has Male in it?
She has He in it?
Madam had Adam in it?
Why do all women's problems start with Men?
MENtal illness, MENtal breakdown, MENopause,
GUYnaecologist, and . . .
When we have REAL trouble, it's a HISterectomy!

Author unknown

# Dora Bryan

Dora Bryan, one of the UK's favourite actresses, recently celebrated more than 70 years in showbusiness. Starting her career in 1935 at the Palace Theatre in Manchester when she was just 12, today Dora still manages to do the same tap dance and splits that she did then.

Although Dora is often seen as one of the funniest ladies on television, her career seems to have spanned every conceivable style in theatre, television and films around the world. By the time Dora was 37, she had featured in 28 films and her classic role in *A Taste of Honey* earned her a BAFTA for Best Actress in 1961. Her stunning performance in the long-running *Hello Dolly* at the Theatre Royal, Drury Lane, was another highlight in Dora's glittering career. She even had a chart hit with 'All I Want for Christmas is a Beatle', appearing on *Top of the Pops* in 1963. The song is still played every Christmas.

Dora says that her faith and trust in God has got her through the toughest of times, including the pain and tragedy of seeing her adopted daughter Georgina die of alcohol abuse, and the loss of her husband, Bill. Despite the difficulties, and the many unanswered questions, God has remained at the heart of Dora's life and work.

'Knowing I am loved by God makes it easy to pray. I am a great believer in prayer and I pray all the time, whether I'm about to go on stage or wash up. I love talking to God.'

## A Simple Thank You

Dear Lord,
Thank you for revealing yourself to me. Thank you for all I have and for teaching me that love is all that matters. Please help me each day to be a good witness for you in this way. Amen.

## Unanswered Prayer

I asked for strength that I might achieve;
I was made weak that I might learn humbly to obey.
I asked for health that I might do greater things;
I was given infirmity that I might do better things.
I asked for riches that I might be happy;
I was given poverty that I might be wise.
I asked for power that I might have the praise of men;

I was given weakness that I might feel the need of God.
I asked for all things that I might enjoy life;
I was given life that I might enjoy all things.
I got nothing that I had asked for,
but everything that I had hoped for.
Almost despite myself my unspoken prayers were
    answered;
I am, among all men, most richly blessed. Amen.

Prayer of an unknown Confederate soldier

## John Byrne

John Byrne has been the career adviser for *The Stage* news-paper for the past five years, alongside his own career as a writer, broadcaster and children's performer with his 'Live Stand Up Cartooning' workshops.

Via his popular 'Dear John' column, as well as in private sessions with performers young and old and in lectures and seminars at venues ranging from the Guildhall to the Edinburgh Festival, John's focus is on helping performers develop the business side of their showbusiness career. It's still an area John feels is often shrouded in mystery, outdated information and, sadly, sometimes open to outright exploitation.

'Talking to so many performers about the nitty-gritty of their careers is a great privilege,' John says, 'but it doesn't necessarily make me an expert. Actually it just reminds me all the more how much we all need God's grace to get through each day. Despite what the TV talent shows would have you believe, for most of us keeping a showbusiness career on the road is not the result of any "X, Y or Z Factor" but more a constant process of doing our best with the talents we have got in small ways day in and day out. I'm constantly humbled by the way in which some of the biggest and best-known stars who have come up by that long, hard route are more than willing to share their experiences and knowledge with beginners.

'As the saying goes, "You want fame? Well, fame costs." My prayer is one to remind me that on the days when it seems to be costing more than I can bear, help is close at hand from the One who has already paid the price for all of us.'

The following is John's own prayer:

## Help at Hand

It's a hard business but you are my protector.
It's a lonely business yet you're with me every day.
It's an 'image' business but you love the me behind the make-up.
It's Showbusiness . . . thank you, Lord, for showing me the way.

There is an amusing cartoon strip in which a tiny insect is looking up at a much larger specimen. 'What kind of insect are you?' asks the puzzled little bug. 'I'm a praying mantis,' is the reply. 'That's absurd,' says the tiny bug. 'Insects don't pray!' Whereupon the praying mantis grabs the tiny bug by the throat and begins to squeeze. Caught in this desperate situation, his bulging eyes rolling heavenward, the tiny bug says, 'Our Father, who art in heaven . . .'

## Jason Carter

Jason Carter has become a cultural and global ambassador, having performed in over 70 countries, including some of the least accessible places – such as North Korea, Afghanistan, Saudi Arabia, Iran, Pakistan and Uzbekistan – often supported by the British government. He has also received music awards from the government of North Korea and the Crown Prince of Bahrain, acknowledging Jason's efforts to 'build bridges' through music.

Jason has recorded 14 CDs, and his tracks have appeared on compilations alongside numerous artists such as Anoushka Shankar, Barbra Streisand, Ozzy Osbourne and John Paul Jones from Led Zeppelin. Jason is Peace Ambassador with Café Diplo, a humanitarian organization dedicated to spreading the message of peace through the arts; however contemporary his music, his choice of prayer dates back many years.

'This well-known hymn has stayed with me since early schooldays,' Jason explains, 'and even as a seven-year-old boy these words have meant so much to me. It was recently revived in my heart when I performed at Repton School in Derby. The original tune by Hubert Parry was written in 1888, but in 1924 Dr George Gilbert Stocks, director of music at Repton School, set it to the familiar tune we know today, for use in the school chapel. To perform in the same place that Stocks had worked resonated deep within me.

'It's interesting how we are so used to singing these old hymns, but often forget to take the words in properly as we sing them. Perhaps in the form of a prayer, it's easier to let the meaning soak into our spirits?'

## Dear Lord and Father of Mankind

Dear Lord and Father of mankind,
Forgive our foolish ways;
Reclothe us in our rightful mind;
In purer lives thy service find,
In deeper reverence, praise.
In simple trust like theirs who heard
Beside the Syrian sea
The gracious calling of the Lord,
Let us, like them, without a word

Rise up and follow thee.
Drop thy still dews of quietness,
Till all our strivings cease;
Take from our souls the strain and stress,
And let our ordered lives confess
The beauty of thy peace.
Breathe through the heats of our desire
Thy coolness and thy balm;
Let sense be dumb, let flesh retire;
Speak through the earthquake, wind and fire,
O still small voice of calm!

John Whittier, 1872

## Prayer for the Unemployed Actor

Oh Great Director-in-the-Sky
Do you ever look down and wonder why?
I flip them burgers night and day;
Sell appliances to make ends meet;
Hand out flyers on the street.
Help my dream come to fruition;
Let me win just one audition!
It doesn't have to be for major bucks;
But hey, God, sometimes, my life sucks!
Residuals sure would mean a lot;
I'd pay back all these bills I've got,
Buy human food instead of Spam,
Buy new clothes instead of second hand.
I'm not looking for mass adoration;
Just a little less humiliation.
And a new set of headshots
so I don't look so fat . . .

Oh and by the way:
Would you like fries with that?

Richard Bischoff

## Charlie Case

Charlie Case is known as one of the best all-rounders in the business. He has entertained at the highest levels of fun, including celebrity parties, Harrods, and even Number 10 Downing Street. He is also a brilliant clown and, as you would expect, he has enjoyed some hilarious moments while entertaining.

He was on his way to do his Christmas Day party at the Hilton Hotel at Gatwick when he decided to stop and tidy up his clown make-up just before the show. Sitting in his car just outside the airport's perimeter fence, he was suddenly surrounded by police marksmen and security personnel.

They thought he was a clown terrorist, and were just about to arrest him when Charlie told them a few of his favourite Christmas cracker jokes and they immediately knew he was a real clown. It's one of the funniest things that's ever happened to him and made his Christmas Day unforgettable!

Charlie also remembers, 'Years ago I was booked to do a summer season in Yarmouth and I thought it would be a great opportunity for me to pop into Anglia Television nearby on my day off and introduce myself as a budding children's presenter. I had a fabulous idea to get myself noticed by wearing a duck outfit and so I parked the car across the road from the studios, struggled into the costume complete with beak, feathers and webbed feet, and waddled across the road to the sound of screeching cars and horns. I'm being noticed at last, I thought! When I fumbled my way into the reception the girl behind the desk didn't even look up. She probably had strange men dressed as ducks walking into the studio every day, it seemed. "We don't have a children's department here," she bellowed without even looking up, and so I just turned around and waddled straight out again.

'This is a prayer that my wife, Sue, wrote in the form of a poem . . .'

## It's All Worthwhile

I woke up this morning, what am I doing today?
I've got a show in Brighton, I must get under way.
Choose a coloured T-shirt, maybe red, maybe blue,
Maybe yellow, maybe green, no, the orange one will do.

I chose the spotty trousers, they end halfway up my calf,
With different coloured socks on, that should make them
   laugh.
I've got some purple boots, for me they're much too big,
But with their yellow laces, I just don't give a fig.

The next thing that I have to do
Is paint my cheeks a rosy hue.
I love slapping on my happy mouth –
Corners turning northwards, not turning south.

I put lots of white around my eyes,
And draw my eyebrows to twice their size.
With that palaver out of the way
I stick on a big red nose, and hope it will stay.

I load up the car with all my props –
Bails, hoops, puppets and spinning tops.
I always leave early because I know
There will be traffic jams, road works, and stop and go.

I arrive at the venue, unload the car,
People are coming from near and far.
It certainly makes it all seem worthwhile,
When I see so many people start to smile.

Each day I know that I've been blessed.
What do I do, can you guess?
A gift from God, he made me a clown.
I cheer people up when they feel down.
The pleasure I give, bounces back to me.
So thank you, Lord, for making me, me!

Dear God,
Instead of letting people die and having to make new
ones, why don't you just keep the ones you already have?

Cindy, aged six

## Fiona Castle

Fiona Castle is the widow of Roy Castle, the popular television entertainer. She is author of several books and compiler of a number of anthologies. She is involved with the Roy Castle Lung Cancer Foundation and also works to empower Christian women in seminars and workshops.

'So many of my prayers are off the cuff!' Fiona says. 'I always say that the most amazing prayer for me to get my head round comes from Jesus' "High priestly prayer" in John 17. He is praying to his Father for his disciples, and continues by saying:

I am praying not only for these disciples but also for all who will ever believe in me because of their testimony. My prayer for all of them is that they will be one, just as you and I are one, Father – that just as you are in me and I am in you, so they will be in us and the world will believe you sent me.

'How wonderful that Jesus, all those centuries ago, was praying for you and me. It was only because the disciples gave their lives to tell the good news to the next generations that we have the privilege of knowing it today. Now the responsibility is ours to do the same for the coming generation, so that they will know the love of Jesus in their lives. What a huge challenge! We need to pray for courage to continue to make the love of Jesus known today.

'A prayer which has stayed with me since my childhood was the school prayer when I went to Elmhurst Ballet School, a boarding school, at the age of nine. It has stood me in good stead over the years as I have put this prayer into practice, to give me the courage to keep on keeping on, without growing weary or discouraged!'

## Prayer for Courage

Teach us, good Lord, to serve Thee as Thou deservest.
To give and not to count the cost,
to fight and not to heed the wounds;

to toil and not to seek for rest;
to labour and not to ask for any reward,
save that of knowing that we do Thy holy will. Amen.

Ignatius, 1556

Johnny had been misbehaving and was sent to his room.
After a while he emerged and informed his mother that
he had thought it over and then said a prayer. 'Fine,' said
the pleased mother. 'If you ask God to help you not to
misbehave, he will help you.' 'Oh, I didn't ask him to
help me not to misbehave,' said Johnny. 'I asked him to
help you put up with me.'

# Wendy Craig

Wendy Craig, seen recently appearing in the eighth series
of ITV's *The Royal*, was already famous for her role as
a mother in a series of television shows, and recalls that
the funniest moments of *Butterflies* were when her hopeless cooking brought constant consternation from her TV
family.

'Such lines as "Must you peer like that?" brought howls of
laughter from audiences as my character placed yet another
burnt cinder of a dish before them. The burnt food became
a sort of hinge point in the series. Horrid food, lumpy cus-
tard, steamed puddings that were like rocks, were all part
of the everyday menu, and became a running gag. We had
a good laugh acting it all out, and encouraged writer Carla

Lane to put some frightful mishap in the show each week. If Ben, Ria and the boys had bowed their heads before eating the meal, perhaps they would have said something like this funny prayer.'

## Hypochondriac's Grace

Dear Lord, we ask you if you will,
put your blessing on this meal.
We ask you, Father, if it pleases,
protect us from these new diseases.
Please bless the spinach, and the romaine.
And cleanse it of some lurking ptomaine.
God, bless our ice cream and our cola.
Pray it's not teeming with Ebola.
And pray the deli didn't sell us
coleslaw ripe with salmonellas.
We also ask a special blessing:
no botulism in the dressing.
While we regard your higher power,
make sure the devilled eggs aren't sour.
And please, Lord, bless our sirloin tip,
and purge it of E Coli's grip.
A special blessing on the sherry,
oh Lord, we need no dysentery,
so it not poisons, nor impacts,
nor liquefies our lower tracts.
And Lord, make sure no one is able
to get sick and die upon this table.
So bless, Lord, all this food we share.
Ensure no deadly virus there.
And once we're full and satiated,
we pray we aren't all contaminated,
and wind up just another toll

for the Centre for Disease Control.
One last thing, Lord, if it's OK,
please hold this blessing that we pray.
For all this fear, and all this fright,
has made us lose our appetite.

Fred Moore

Wendy says, 'The following song came to me one day while walking in the countryside with my dog. I was asking God for his guidance, and as I was praying I began to sing. The tune and the words came to me out of the blue, and when I got home I could still remember them. I sang them on to a cassette, and my son Ross transcribed them and wrote a simple arrangement for me.

'Years later I spoke the words on BBC's *Songs of Praise* accompanied by my son Alaster on the oboe, and I was overwhelmed at the response from viewers who felt the lyrics touched their own thoughts and feelings. It is a simple request to God to show me the way.'

## Show Me the Way

When I'm confused, Lord, show me the way
Show me, show me, show me the way
Baffled and bruised, Lord, show me the way
Show me, show me, show me the way

Still my heart and clear my mind
Prepare my soul to hear
Your still, small voice
Your word of truth
Peace be still your Lord is here
Always so close to show you the way
Show you, show you, show you the way

When I'm afraid, Lord, show me the way
Show me, show me, show me the way
Weak and dismayed, Lord, show me the way
Show me, show me, show me the way

Lift my spirit with your love
Bring courage, calm and peace
You who bore all for my sake
So I could walk from fear released
With you beside me
Showing the way
Showing, showing, showing the way

One Sunday a young child was 'acting up' during the morning service. The parents did their best to maintain some sense of order in the pew, but were losing the battle. Finally, the father picked the little fellow up and walked sternly up the aisle on his way out. Just before reaching the safety of the foyer, the little one called loudly to the congregation, 'Pray for me! Pray for me!'

# Jimmy Cricket

Jimmy Cricket is famed for his catchphrase 'And there's more', but there really is more to Jimmy than meets the eye. With his special brand of family humour, Jimmy has enjoyed great success on stage, television and radio. 'There are enough long faces in the world, and I don't plan to become one of them!' says Jimmy. He sees laughter as a very important release valve, and his job is to open it, as wide as possible.

Jimmy was born into a large Irish family, with four brothers and one sister. His father was an undertaker by trade, but had a wonderful sense of humour and the house was always filled with laughter. Their house was also filled with the reality of God. Very much a God-fearing family, they would attend church each Sunday on a regular basis, and Jimmy realizes that this is where his faith first took root.

'I work in such a dodgy profession and the old show-business saying "Don't ring us, we'll ring you" is quite true, and sometimes you never really know when the phone is going to ring. That goes for stars and chorus girls alike – one minute you are in great demand and the next you wonder what the future holds. I never really know what the future holds, but I do know who holds the future!'

## Cricket's Prayer

Heavenly Father, help me to relax when times are hard, and know that there's a higher power guiding me.
Give me the serenity to smile through the lean times,
give me the faith and confidence to know that if I do my best for you, everything else will be taken care of.
And most of all, help me to use the talent you have given me to enrich people's lives with love and laughter.
Through your son, Jesus Christ. Amen.

## The Single Female Prayer

Before I lay me down to sleep,
I pray for a man who's not a creep,
One who's handsome, smart and strong,
One who loves to listen long,
One who thinks before he speaks,
One who'll call, not wait for weeks.
I pray he's gainfully employed,
When I spend his cash, won't be annoyed.
Pulls out my chair and opens my door,
Massages my back and begs to do more.
Oh! Send me a man who'll make love to my mind,
Knows what to answer to 'How big is my behind?'
I pray that this man will love me no end,
and always want to be my friend. Amen.

Author unknown

## Rosemary Conley

Rosemary Conley CBE is the UK's leading diet and fitness expert, with more than 40 years' experience. Most recently, she has starred in the second series of a primetime ITV 1 show, *Slim to Win with Rosemary Conley*.

The Rosemary Conley approach is characterized by a low-fat diet regime, and her classes also offer a 45-minute aerobic workout with a trained instructor. Thus it provides a fitness club for people wanting an alternative to gym membership rather than simply another 'fat club' for dieters, although there are similar product endorsements of foods and kitchen equipment. Rosemary has presented over 400 cookery programmes on television as well as presenting her own series on both the BBC and ITV in addition to appearing on *This Morning* with Richard and Judy for seven years. She continues to have a high media profile with many regular appearances on national radio and television.

'I became a Christian in 1986 when I asked God into my life,' Rosemary explains. 'I surrendered totally to him and from that moment on I have tried to live my life his way – not mine!

'There were no blinding flashes of light or cracks of thunder or puffs of smoke when I asked Jesus into my life, but I know that as soon as I had prayed, kneeling at the side of my bed, something very dramatic had happened. I had no idea my life would change so dramatically in the years that followed.

'While I have enjoyed great success with my books, videos, diet and fitness clubs and magazine, none of it could have been achieved without the blessing of the Lord. He gave me the energy, the ideas, the opportunities, and the humility to realize that what I had achieved was God's own gift.

'One of the most dramatic changes in how I felt was the most unbelievable amount of love towards my husband, my daughter and towards my fellow human beings. I know that this is God's love reaching through me to touch others. We cannot survive in this world without love and the feeling that we are loved.

'Amazingly, the more we love others the more love they give back – perhaps that is one of the greatest things I have learned since becoming a Christian. I remember at first being very worried that I didn't know how to serve the Lord. Then one day, after having a chat with a minister, and his reassurance that the Lord would tell me in his own good time what he wanted me to do, I felt more relaxed. Extraordinarily, as I drove home after that very conversation I turned on the radio and the next song to be played was Cliff Richard and Sarah Brightman singing that beautiful song from *The Phantom of the Opera*, "All I Ask of You". The lyrics sang out what I believed was my message from the Lord – "All I ask of you is that you love me". In my mind it was so clear that this was the message that was being given to me and I was elated because I felt yes, I could do that easily.

'This was a turning point for me. Every day I try to remember to tell the Lord, as well as my husband, that I love him. Love is something that we should never take for granted, but to know that the Lord Jesus loves us more than we could ever love him, should be one of the greatest comforts we will ever experience. It is his love at work through us that enables me to face each day determined to help others in whatever way he shows. This prayer combines the one that I prayed in 1986 when I asked God into my life with one I try to pray every day.'

## Your Way

Lord,
I've been living my life my own way.
Now I want to live it your way.
Come, Lord, and occupy the throne of my life.
Make me the kind of person you want me to be.
Thank you for your abounding love, your patience and your
    forgiveness.
You hold no record of wrongs and I am grateful that you
    showed me the way to love you.
I love you, Lord, and I ask you to make me the person that
    you want me to be.

Help me, Lord, to be more like you.
Help me to serve you in serving others. Amen.

# Dana

Dana became a household name in 1970 when the young schoolgirl from Derry won the Eurovision Song Contest with 'All Kinds of Everything'. Enjoying a string of hits and TV shows throughout the 1970s and 1980s, she won numerous awards and was voted best female artist. In 1999 she was elected as Member of the European Parliament and her popular autobiography was published in 2008. She has recently made a welcome return to the UK stage and is enjoying performing for her many fans once more.

Dana loved being a mum and still has fond memories of being pregnant: 'Until I saw the scan of the baby within me, I didn't truly realize that there was life within me. I knew it in my head but actually seeing it with my eyes brought about an awareness that I hadn't communicated with the child. All I had been thinking about was me, my motherhood, and Damien and I as parents. I wanted to do something to change this and so I felt I should talk and pray with this little person, so I made up this prayer lullaby to sing to him or her.'

## Lullaby to the Unborn

Little baby yet unborn
In my womb so safe and warm.
Living with me, who will you be?

Living with me, I wish I could see,
My little baby yet unborn,
In my womb so safe and warm.

Dear God,
So far today, I've done all right.
I haven't lost my temper, haven't been grumpy, nasty, selfish or overindulgent.
I'm glad of that, but in a few minutes, God, I'm going to get out of bed and from there on I'm going to need a lot more help.
Thanking you in advance. Amen.

## Brian D'Arcy

Brian D'Arcy is the presenter of *Sunday Half Hour*, BBC Radio 2's weekly programme of hymns and prayers. As the current Superior of The Graan, Enniskillen, Brian is one of Ireland's best-known and best-loved priests. He is a native of Bellanaleck, Enniskillen, in Northern Ireland, entered The Graan in 1962, and was ordained a priest in 1969.

An accomplished author, newspaper columnist, broadcaster, journalist and chaplain to the entertainment industry, he is the first priest in Ireland to be admitted to the National Union of Journalists. He has served as editor of *The Cross* magazine, production editor of the Catholic Communications Centre in Dublin, Parish Priest of Mount Argus, and Superior in Crossgar before returning to The Graan as Superior.

He has his own music programme, *Sunday with Brian D'Arcy*, on BBC Radio Ulster, and is a well-loved contributor to Radio 2's 'Pause For Thought' on *Wake Up To Wogan*. In Terry Wogan's words, 'He epitomizes everything that a man of God should be.'

Father Brian has broadcast for Ireland's RTE radio and television for 40 years. His published memoirs *A Different Journey* is a Number 1 bestseller, and his most recent book, *Through the Year with Brian D'Arcy*, is one he was asked to write many times by his numerous fans. The book is comprised of 365 thoughts and reflections to accompany the reader every day throughout the year.

Brian has chosen the following as his favourite prayer:

## Where Am I Going?

My Lord God, I have no idea where I am going,
I do not see the road ahead of me.
I cannot know for certain where it will end.
Nor do I really know myself, and the fact that I think I am following Your will does not mean that I am actually doing so.
But I believe that the desire to please You does in fact please You.

And I hope that I have that desire in all that I am doing.
I hope that I will never do anything apart from that desire.
And I know that if I do this, You will lead me by the right
   road,
Though I may know nothing about it.
Therefore I will trust You always though
I may seem to be lost and in the shadow of death.
I will not fear, for You are ever with me,
And You will never leave me to face my perils alone.

Prayer by Thomas Merton, cited in A Different Journey by
Brian D'Arcy

**Alexander Whyte**, the famous Scottish preacher, invariably began his public prayers with an expression of gratitude. One cold and rainy day when his people wondered how he could be grateful for the weather, he began by saying, 'We thank Thee, O Lord, that it is not always like this!'

# Janie Dee

Janie Dee, the multi-award-winning actress, must be one of the most versatile performers currently on the British stage. She started her professional life as a dancer on the end of a pier, moved into musicals, and then developed a career as an actress in straight plays. To prove her love of variety and ability to cope with any challenge, she produced the London Concert for Peace. Appearing many times on the London stage, her performance in Alan Ayckbourn's play *Comic*

*Potential* earned her Best Actress awards at the Oliviers, *Evening Standard* and Critics Circle, the three most prestigious awards British theatre can bestow, an achievement only matched by Dame Judi Dench.

Recently, Janie played the role of Joyce Gresham opposite Charles Dance in *Shadowlands*, the moving play that charts the extraordinary love story between Joy Gresham and C. S. Lewis. The play, which explores love, faith and the fragility of human happiness with great grace and generosity, offered Janie a difficult and multi-layered character to explore as well as her own personal faith. Janie explains, 'Joy is a Jewish, communist, American, Christian . . . who was converted to Christianity through reading C. S. Lewis's work. She was probably better read than C. S. Lewis, which is really saying something. It has been very stressful. I remember three nights when I didn't sleep because I thought I'm not getting this part and I've got to do something, I've got to find her, it's no good blaming the director, he can't tell me. On the third night, I was up all night and I suddenly thought of the idea of what she looked like. Every intellectual you meet, every bookish person you meet, has spectacles, they just do because they're using their eyes so much.'

Janie is married to actor Rupert Wickman and her home life is just as important to her as her stage career: 'The moment that changed me for ever was giving birth to my daughter. I was so in awe of what had just happened, and it immediately put everything into perspective.

'People often say to me, "How do you manage, having a career as well as children?" I say to them, I don't know how I would manage without both. Having children and a passion in your life, apart from your family – which of course is a big passion, an equal passion – but having a focus that really excites you – in my case acting and singing – if that is your other focus then you'll probably find that you have more energy. When I have been at home, simply going round and round the house doing the housework and it just never finishes, I find it much more tiring and much more debilitating as a woman, to do just that all the time. I think it's really, really, really hard and everybody underestimates what that can do to your mind.

'If I was asked to describe my life in six words they would be: happy, challenging, creative, chaotic, stimulating and blessed.' Janie has chosen to adopt the following prayer for those who lead busy lives.

## Life's Prayer

Lord, support us all day long
until shadows lengthen,
evening comes,
the busy world hushed,
the fever of life is over
and our life's work is done.

From *The Book of Common Prayer*

Janie adds, 'I feel I should also add my own prayer that I say every night before the curtain goes up. Maybe it's too chatty, but it is more or less exactly what I say every night to God before the performance . . .'

## Bless Everyone Here

Dear Lord,
Please bless everyone here tonight:
the audience, the cast, all those
working front of house and

behind the scenes.
Bring your love and light to us
so that we may understand where you are
and where you are not,
and how we fail to find you sometimes
even though you are always there.
Thank you, Lord, for this life.
Guide me always.
Amen.

During the minister's prayer one Sunday, there was a loud whistle from one of the back pews. Gary's mother was horrified. She pinched him into silence and, after church, asked, 'Gary, whatever made you do such a thing?' Gary answered soberly, 'I asked God to teach me to whistle . . . And he did just then!'

## Ken Dodd

Ken Dodd was born in a farmhouse on the outskirts of Liverpool in a place called Knotty Ash. The rest, as they say, is history! A singer in his local church choir, the seven-year-old took a bet to ride his bike with his eyes closed, and the resulting crash caused the famous teeth that became his trademark. Working hard during the day as a door-to-door salesman, Ken performed his comedy act Professor Yaffle Chuckabutty in the clubs at night. After inventing The Diddymen in 1959 he eventually became a household name in 1965 and broke all box office records at the London Palladium, and sold millions of his top recording hits. Doddy is in the *Guinness Book of Records* for the longest joke-telling time: a mammoth 1,500 jokes in three and a half hours. Ken is seen by his peers as one of the finest comedy performers of all time. He recently celebrated 50 years at the top of his profession in a recent BBC TV *Songs of Praise* special. Ken says about *Songs of Praise*, 'It was a great privilege to be asked and a wonderful experience. I was allowed to choose the hymns, and I picked all good tunes. I was a choirboy – until they found out where the noise was coming from.'

Ken says that laughter is a divine gift. 'It's like jogging on the inside,' he says. Doddy still tours to sell-out crowds all over the country, and never forgets the one who gave him the gift of making us laugh.

'My favourite short prayer is the Grace.'

The Grace of our Lord Jesus Christ and the love of God and the fellowship of the Holy Spirit be with us evermore. Amen.

Doddy, known as the comedian's comic, also suggests that the following prayer can be adopted by all of us . . .

## The Clown's Prayer

As I stumble through this life,
help me to create more laughter than tears,
dispense more happiness than gloom,
spread more cheer than despair.
Never let me become so indifferent
that I will fail to see the wonder
in the eyes of a child
or the twinkle in the eyes of the aged.

Never let me forget that my total effort
is to cheer people, make them happy
and forget – at least momentarily –
all the unpleasantness in their lives.
And, in my final moment,
may I hear You whisper:
'When you made My people smile,
you made Me smile.'

Author unknown

A small five-year-old boy was in the kitchen trying,
unsuccessfully, to kill an insect with a broom. Apparently,
the best he could do was stun the bug, because – after
some time – he prayed, 'That bug thinks he's Jesus! . . .
'cause I keep killing him and he keeps coming back alive!'

## Mike Doyle

Mike Doyle's unique blend of brilliant comedy, matched
with a truly fantastic singing voice, has made him one of
the UK's top entertainers.

'I love the Bible story about the Prodigal Son because it
makes me think of my own son,' Mike explains. 'When he's
had a bad day he gets cross, throws a tantrum, runs up to
his bedroom, and slams the door. It's normally about half
an hour later that he will come slowly down the stairs, sidle
quietly into our front room, and whisper a "Sorry, Daddy"
in my ear.

'So, what do I do? Shout and scream at him to make him feel really bad? Make him do the washing-up for a week? Or tell him to do 20 press-ups? No, of course not! As a father his word of apology makes my heart jump, and almost makes we want to cry because I know he means it, and I love him so much. Hugs all round, and everything is fine between us again.

'It's just like that with my heavenly Daddy too. I know I will fail, I know I'll get cross with God, I even know that I am capable of running away from him. But I also know that he will be there, watching and waiting for me to return, ready to hear me say a humble "Sorry".

'Does he holler at me and send huge punishment down on me? No, though it's possible that my actions may have some other effect, he wraps his arms around me, and welcomes me back home. Some mistakes I seem to make over and over again, and yet I know he's always ready to forgive.'

## Getting It Wrong

Dear Father, help me never to forget that no matter how many times I get it wrong, you are always there to hear my words of apology and welcome me back into your arms. Help me to forgive others in the same way too. Amen.

'Aren't children wonderful? Fourteen years ago I was pregnant and the due date was a week or two after my oldest daughter's birthday. One day my oldest asked, "Mummy, can you have that baby on my birthday and can it be a girl?" I told her only God could control that. She started praying, and on her birthday, a Sunday, we went to church, a friend arranged a party for my daughter, after which I went to the hospital and gave birth to a baby girl! 10.23p.m. God is GOOD!'

# Bella Emberg

Bella Emberg is best known and loved as the comedy female side-kick in Russ Abbot's many *Madhouse* television series. She has also appeared in countless comedy seasons, tours and pantomimes across the UK and was recently seen in BBC TV's *Doctor Who*.

## To Understand

Dear God,
Please give me the patience to understand the younger generation, not to be so quick to judge, and to remind me that I was once young.
Amen.

Dear God,
Why is Sunday School on Sunday? I thought it was supposed to be our day of rest?

Tom, aged eight

# John Forrest

John Forrest, television producer/director, has created many editions of BBC TV's *Songs of Praise*. Apart from producing many of their biggest TV specials, John was responsible for the Ken Dodd 50th anniversary programme, and after making one with Clowns International they even made John an honorary member! This prayer is John's own, written as if seen through a camera lens.

## Gifts

Lord, thank you for the brilliant gifts you've given to the
   people you've created.
Thank you for the joy of laughter,
The thrill of music,
The challenge of drama
And the excitement of movement.

Thank you for colour
And sound,
For rhythm and shape.

Help us to be creative
In ways which show the world
How it can be the place you want it to be.

Help us create some works of art and entertainment so good
That everyone who sees them
Will want to glorify you, our God.
Amen.

A five-year-old said grace at family dinner one night. 'Dear God, thank you for these pancakes . . .' When he concluded, his parents asked him why he thanked God for pancakes when they were having chicken. The boy smiled and said, 'I thought I'd see if God was paying attention tonight.'

## Steve Fortune

Steve Fortune is an all-round performer with a 30-year career to date. Alongside his television roles, he has appeared in London's West End many times, in such productions as *Fiddler on the Roof*, *Underneath the Arches*, and in panto-mime at the Old Vic.

It was the birth of Steve's son that brought him and his wife Tracy into the church and into a relationship with God, and it is quite interesting to note that in the same year Steve was cast in the revival of Andrew Lloyd Webber's and Tim Rice's production of *Jesus Christ Superstar*, which re-opened London's Lyceum Theatre after a gap of 25 years.

How did Steve feel about being in such a show? 'Well, as a Christian it was an opportunity through the medium of theatre to tell the story of the Passion. Although previous productions of the show had possibly trivialized the story, the director of this new production, Gale Edwards, wanted it to be more realistic and moving. The response from people who have seen the show has confirmed that it is very thought-provoking, and indeed has caused a number of people to re-examine their own feelings.

'There have been criticisms of the show and certain liberties have been taken with the gospel for dramatic reasons. For example, many of the actions associated with women have been grouped together and attributed to Mary Magdalene, but this is theatrical licence, and if at the end of the show people go away thinking about the life and awful death of Christ on the cross then surely the show is "shining as a light to the world" and that can't be a bad thing.

'We are called by God to live as he would have us live and the doorway by which we enter that life is through love.'

## A Prayer for Love

Grant, O Lord, that your unimaginable love
May find in me some love to meet it.
Let me love the love that ever loves me.
Let my soul's delight be to love you
And what you love,
And whom you love,
Now and always, life without end.
Through your son, Jesus Christ.
Amen.

Author unknown

Steve is also an accomplished writer and recently he really enjoyed writing his first pantomime, *Dick Whittington*: 'Every year the gospel is enacted on stage at Christmas and New Year in the form of this wonderful, traditional family entertainment. Good always defeats the baddie to the re-sounding cheers of an appreciative and relieved audience. Like the life that pantomime parodies, I am often concerned for the stress we encounter in our everyday lives and offer this serious-looking prayer with a touch of humour.'

## A Prayer for the Stressed

Dear Lord,

Grant me the serenity to accept the things I cannot change, the courage to change the things I cannot accept, and the wisdom to hide the bodies of those I had to kill today, because they got on my nerves.

And also help me to be careful of the toes I step on today, as they may be connected to the feet I may have to kiss tomorrow.

Help me always to give 100% at work . . .

12% on Monday
23% on Tuesday
40% on Wednesday
20% on Thursday
and 5% on Friday

And help me to remember . . .

When I'm having a bad day and it seems people are trying to wind me up, it takes 42 muscles to frown, 28 to smile – and only four to extend my arm and smack someone in the mouth! Amen.

Author unknown

Three preachers sat discussing the best positions for prayer, while a telephone repairman worked nearby.

'Kneeling is definitely best,' claimed one.

'No,' another contended. 'I get the best results standing with my hands outstretched to heaven.'

'You're both wrong,' the third insisted. 'The most effective prayer position is lying prostrate, face down on the floor.'

The repairman could contain himself no longer.

'Gentlemen,' he interrupted, 'the best praying I ever did was hanging upside down from a telegraph pole.'

## Phillip Griffiths

Phillip Griffiths must be one of the longest-serving members of London's West End. He has been in a variety of productions since 1978, and not only is he currently appearing in Andrew Lloyd Webber's *The Phantom of the Opera*, but he has been in that production for the past 18 years.

Having toured with most of the UK's leading opera companies, doing the same show night after night is something Phillip has got quite used to now. Instead of being bored, however, he finds that the different audience every night brings some measure of freshness to each performance.

*Evita*, Tim Rice's and Andrew Lloyd Webber's musical, opened in 1978 and ran for 2,900 performances. The whole country had been buzzing with excitement, waiting to see what was said to be a landmark musical phenomenon. Indeed it was. The huge metal set, the lit floor, the brilliant lyrics and score, but above all it was the subject-matter that caught the audience's imagination. Gone were the dancing girls of the traditional musical; here was the story of one woman's phenomenal rise to power, and her tragic death.

Phillip remembers that the show started with a funeral and finished with a funeral, which, while the audiences applauded, didn't help the cast to feel very exhilarated. In fact, some of the cast became depressed, and at one time, after a member of the cast had committed suicide, it was said that there was even a curse on the theatre.

It was during this time that two new cast members joining the show happened to be Christians. They both felt the atmosphere at the theatre to be very heavy, and both prayed individually for support and fellowship. Imagine their surprise when one day they discovered each other's faith through a book by Billy Graham having been left on a dressing-room table. Immediately they knew their prayers had been answered, and started to meet together each week in their dressing room.

Theatres are small communities where gossip is often rife, and it didn't take long for the rest of the theatre, and eventually the entire West End, to hear about this strange Christian meeting going on backstage at the Prince Edward Theatre.

Despite having been brought up in a Christian home, Phillip found his faith had recently become a little stale, finding it too easy to leave God in church every Sunday. He had heard about the new weekly meeting, but had decided to stay away. Describing himself as the doubting Thomas, he had imagined that a backstage Bible study was probably the most boring thing around. When he heard other members of the cast talking enthusiastically about the time they had spent together, he decided to give it a try. When he joined in the following week, Phillip was delighted. It was not as he imagined; this was something different. It was interesting, personal and very exciting. Here was an opportunity to see the relevance of God right here in his place of work.

The small group that met each week soon expanded from three to, at one stage, thirteen. Phillip found the Bible study, teaching and especially the prayer a great source of help, inspiration and encouragement. By now many different people from many West End theatres were cramming into the tiny backstage room, and it was here no more than a year later, in 1982, that Phillip became one of the founder members of the new organization Christians in Entertainment.

Many of the cast on *Evita* commented on the fact that the atmosphere at the theatre had changed, and that the show seemed much easier to work on. In the end, *Evita* ran for nearly eight years, and Phillip likes to think that God's special involvement may have had something to do with the success it enjoyed.

'Have you ever felt that your prayers are just hitting the ceiling? So have I,' Phillip says. 'But God knows what we are capable of, and he understands how hard it is for us to trust him sometimes. The most difficult times are when he seems to be silent.

'God also knows that we forget so easily, so he repeats things to us again and again. That is why this famous hymn is important to me as a prayer. It's reminding me that even when it doesn't seem like it, God is watching over us, and he does hear our prayers. It's a promise that he will never break. Hang on to it!'

## What a Friend We Have in Jesus

What a friend we have in Jesus,
all our sins and grief to bear!
What a privilege to carry
everything to God in prayer!
O what peace we often forfeit,
O what needless pain we bear,
all because we do not carry
everything to God in prayer!

Joseph M. Scriven, 1820–86

46

A rabbi said to a precocious six-year-old boy, 'So your mother says your prayers for you each night? Very commendable. What does she say?' The little boy replied, 'Thank God he's in bed!'

# George Hamilton IV

George Hamilton IV has enjoyed more than 50 years in the music industry, and he's loved every minute of it. From his million-selling songs to his international tours in musicals, the USA's best-loved country music singer became an international pop star with hits such as 'Abilene' and 'Before this Day Ends'.

George is included on the 'Sidewalk to the Stars' at the Country Music Hall of Fame, and *Billboard* magazine gave him the title of International Ambassador of Country Music. Indeed, George Hamilton IV has taken his own special brand of country music to more than 25 countries around the world, and spends many months a year travelling away from his home in Franklin, Tennessee.

However, it is George's love of country gospel music that is closest to his heart, supported by a deep and sincere Christian faith.

George likes nothing more than to sing about his love of Jesus, and many of his secular albums have tracks that are obviously gospel based. He loves touring the UK with his familiar festive concerts based around Easter, Christmas and of course Thanksgiving.

His proudest moments have seen him touring with the best-known Christian evangelist in the world, Billy Graham. On his first date with Billy, it was noted that George won many hearts through his simple, direct and heart-warming songs. It was obvious that what George was singing was really coming from the heart, and coming from God's heart too.

'Worshipping God does not just mean going to church on a Sunday,' George explains. 'We need to worship God all the time, in every place, and in any circumstance. Why? Because when we focus on God, it reminds us who the real boss man is!

'The problem is that sometimes we think we are the boss. In my business, faced with an artiste's insecurity, we often find it easy to hide behind our egos. I work in an industry that is so often absorbed with "self". The star of the show often carries a very heavy responsibility to make the show work. If the box office takings are low, you take it very personally, and wonder if the producer will hire you the next time. The rest of the cast look to you as the leader of the company, so exposing your own insecurities can have the effect of bringing them low too.

'It's true that performers do need confidence to face an audience, though. We have to believe that we really are the best actor, musician, whatever, but if we pretend that our gifts and abilities are of our own making, that's where we start to come unstuck. No, the credit for our talents must go to God, and this verse helps me remember that I must continually offer my talents back to the one who gave them to me in the first place.

'When I speak, think, perform, I try to imagine whether my heavenly Father would be pleased with the way I did it. Every performance I do I offer as a living sacrifice to him. That doesn't mean I always sing gospel songs or talk only about Jesus, I just try to do my best in whatever situation I am in, because I want to please him, in each day that he gives me.'

## Make Us as Instruments

Dear Father,
Make us your instruments,
Like musical instruments that stay in tune with you!
On us, in us and through us,
Play your music – your way! Amen!

Author unknown

A little girl was asked to say grace one day and simply blurted out, 'Rub a dub dub, thanks for the grub!'

# Angela Hardcastle

Angela Hardcastle has extensive experience of dance and choreography within the theatre and television industries, and sees dancing as a spiritual gift to be celebrated.

'Being a Tuesday child with a dancing gift,' she says, 'I have interpreted grace in a physical sense, but it is never divorced from its spiritual meaning as the two are inseparable. I will never be thankful enough for the gift of dancing, and will never do it enough justice.' This is Angela's own prayer:

## Choreographer's Prayer

Connect me with the Music Master,
Pulse of atoms, length of waves,
Rhythmic lover, smoothest mover,
Dancer of seasons and planets and storms.
Let my body find its purpose;
Use my beauties and my faults.
Speed the work and sweeten resting.
Thanks for a lifetime of dancing and grace.

Angela adds, 'Here is another perspective on the spiritual connection to dancing . . .'

## Guidance Is Like a Dance

Dear Lord,
When I meditated on the word Guidance, I kept seeing 'dance' at the end of the word. I remember reading that doing your will is a lot like dancing.

When two people try to lead, nothing feels right. The movement doesn't flow with the music, and everything is quite uncomfortable and jerky. When one person realizes that, and lets the other lead, both bodies begin to flow with the music. One gives gentle cues, perhaps with a nudge to the back or by pressing lightly in one direction or another. It's as if two become one body, moving beautifully.

The dance takes surrender, willingness and attentiveness from one person and gentle guidance and skill from the other.

My eyes drew back to the word Guidance. When I saw 'G', I thought of you, God, followed by 'u' and 'I'. 'God, "u" and "I" dance.'

God, you and I dance. Guidance!
As I bow my head, I am willing to trust that you will offer me guidance about my life. Once again, I became willing to let you lead. Amen.

Author unknown

A little boy was overheard praying: 'Lord, if you can't make me a better boy, don't worry about it. I'm having a really good time like I am!'

## Paul Jones and Fiona Hendley

Paul Jones and Fiona Hendley must be the busiest married couple in showbusiness!

Paul, well known as lead singer of 1960s group Manfred Mann, is remembered for such hits as 'Do Wah Diddy' and 'Pretty Flamingo'. His numerous television appearances include starring as 'Uncle Jack' for the BBC, while millions listen to his programmes on Radio 2 and Jazz FM.

Paul's theatre career ranges from the Royal National Theatre and the Royal Shakespeare Company to the West End and Broadway. He has several Gold discs, stretching from the days of Manfred Mann to the original album of *Evita*, and his own group The Blues Band, which has issued more than 11 albums.

Fiona, an accomplished actress and singer, has worked extensively in all areas of the business, from her acclaimed television series *Widows* to leading roles at the Royal

National Theatre and Royal Shakespeare Company. Fiona is often seen starring in the West End, in a whole range of musicals, drama and comedies.

It was while working together at the Royal National Theatre that Paul and Fiona first met. Without realizing it, they were both on a search for things spiritual too. Paul, a confirmed atheist, was so dogmatic that he had been hired to confront Cliff Richard about his faith on a television debate. However, his hobby of looking at paintings led him eventually to acknowledge that there was another dimension to life: a spiritual one. All his rational, logical and arrogantly intellectual pretences crumbled when he realized that he was dealing with something that actually bypassed all that.

Fiona had been searching for a spiritual meaning to life for some while. Having been originally drawn in by the Moonies cult, she was wary of making any moves towards a standard religion, yet was desperate to discover the truth. Finishing a broadcast for the BBC earlier than expected, Fiona decided to pop into the church next door to Broadcasting House. Enjoying the peaceful atmosphere she opened a nearby Bible and was excited to read a passage that talked about how much God loved people.

In her quest to discover more, Fiona started attending church, with Paul joining her. The opportunity to attend Bible studies, giving them a chance to ask some serious questions about Christian beliefs, was a landmark in their journey. Not long afterwards they were amazed to get a telephone call from the very person Paul had hit out against in that television debate.

Cliff Richard was inviting them to hear an evangelist called Luis Palau. Having heard the evangelist speak so clearly about how they were feeling, they could only agree that God was speaking directly to them, personally. God was answering their plea to know whether he really existed and really cared about them. They found out he not only cared about them but loved them – they received God's love and asked him to be Lord of their lives. They have never regretted it.

Paul explains, 'We don't always know what our day is going to bring, so first thing – before we do anything else – we spend some time with our heavenly Father, telling him about our worries, letting him know that we place our day before him. It really is a fantastic way to start the day!'

This is Paul and Fiona's own prayer:

## Starting the Day

Dearest Father,
Thank you that you love each one of us so much – no matter who we are, or what we've done, no matter where we've come from, or what our background is, your love for us is unconditional. Thank you, Father, that when no one really understands how I feel, you do, because you are my defender and protector, you are my God; in you I trust. When I feel tired and weak, give me strength and energy; when I feel stressed and anxious, show me your peace and calm.

You have promised in your Word that you will never leave me or forsake me. I receive that promise; I receive your mercy, love and kindness. I receive Jesus as Lord and Saviour of my life for ever. Thank you that when I call on you in his name, you answer me and rescue me. I come, Lord, for safety; I remain in you. In Jesus' name. Amen.

Paul and Fiona wrote the following prayer for the new Christians in Entertainment organization some 27 years ago!

## Prayer for Christians in Entertainment

Father,
Thank you that, through your Son Jesus,
I am now aware just how much you love me;
You also gave me talent, a gift to perform.
Oh Lord, put your hand upon all Christians in entertainment
    at this time.
Give us the strength to use that gift to the very best of our
    ability,
and help us to reflect your truth
to all those with whom we are working.
May we glorify your holy name in excellence and love,
for the sake of your Son,
who died for us,
and rose again to
bring us new life.
Amen.

Apparently, we make, on average, 73 decisions a day: 30 of these are work related, 23 are regarding family and relationships, and 11 about a purchase of some sort. No wonder we pray for help in making decisions!

# Jesse Joyner

Jesse Joyner is also known as Jesse the Juggler! Jesse is a normal guy who loves God, his wife Sarah, and juggling – in that order! Since becoming a university graduate and receiving his Master of Divinity Degree, he feels a call to work specifically with families and children. Ever since learning how to juggle in middle school, Jesse has taken his art to places such as Albania, Israel, Los Angeles and New York City. Convinced that Jesus Christ is the only way out of this world's mess, Jesse uses his juggling as a way of talking about God's love.

Jesse is also the President of the Christian Jugglers' Association, an organization that seeks to encourage Christian jugglers in their faith and help them better serve and worship God through their talents. Jesse travels to churches, camps and other events where he entertains with his juggling skills and talks about his experience of God. He recently signed up for a mini-marathon.

'Let me start with a confession,' Jesse says. 'I do not run much. I signed up for a half-marathon as a spontaneous, last-minute whim because my wife, Sarah, was doing the full one and I was tired of watching people do half-marathons and thinking "I could do that". So, without any training or stretching, except the biking that I often do, I got up and ran 13.1 miles. Or rather, slowly jogged. And yes, I was able to juggle the whole time.

'This was my first half-marathon and the furthest I have ever "joggled", or even run, for that matter. I made it all the way to just shy of the 11-mile marker without a stop even for water or to go to the loo. Then it all fell apart. I stopped about four times in miles 11 and 12 and then realized that walking and juggling is harder than joggling (for me at least). There is not a consistent rhythm. It was also hard to get back to running and juggling after having walked. Nonetheless, I picked up and kept going after the four stops and I finished strong with a jog and a run for the last half-mile. I finished in 2.33 and my goal was 2.30. Sarah and I are enjoying limping around the house, and there were some interesting spiritual lessons I picked up along the way!

'I must also make another confession – I love the attention and cheering I get for being a joggler. I love the rush of hearing all those bystanders cheer for me which sends chills through me and gives me enough boosts to make it through the race successfully. It must be like that bit in the Bible that says that the saints in heaven are cheering us on as we run with perseverance the race that is set out before us. If you can joggle as well, then even better. Here's a prayer of mine to help you on your way . . .'

## The Juggler's Prayer

Dear Lord,
you are the great Juggler.

From the celestial bodies to our human bodies, you toss and weave every planet and molecule in a pattern of indescribable beauty.

We can manage only a handful of objects in the air at once.

We can manage only a limited amount of schedules, relationships and responsibilities on this earth.

But you are the eternal, everlasting, all-powerful God, with no limit to your juggling prowess.

May we look to you for all our juggling strength, seeking to emulate the beauty of your patterns in the patterns we make.

We praise you, great Juggler, who is Father, Spirit, and Son – the One True God. Amen.

## Shekhar Kapur

Shekhar Kapur is one of the world's most well-known film directors and one of the few directors who have worked extensively in India's Bollywood film industry as well as in Hollywood.

Kapur started his direction career with a Hindi film, *Masoom*, which went on to win five Filmfare awards, the biggest film awards in India. He then made a breakthrough science-fiction film *Mr India*, which was a huge commercial success, and is considered one of the iconic films of the 1980s in Indian cinema.

He followed this by directing the critically acclaimed *Bandit Queen*, which became an international commercial and critical success; and establishing the Indian Talkies film company with Ram Gopal Varma and Mani Ratnam, two of India's prominent directors. The company produced the film *Dil Se* in 1998 starring Shahrukh Khan, India's biggest star, and is considered one of the best films of Indian cinema.

In 1998, Kapur got international recognition for directing *Elizabeth*, which was nominated for seven Oscars and won Oscar for best make-up. The film also catapulted Cate Blanchett into a major Hollywood star after her portrayal of Queen Elizabeth I.

In 2000, he was awarded India's state honour, the Padma Shri. He directed Heath Ledger in *The Four Feathers* for Paramount/Miramax, and executive produced the Bollywood-themed Andrew Lloyd Webber musical *Bombay Dreams*, which became a very big hit in London's West End and was remade into a Broadway musical in New York.

Kapur, then executive, produced *The Guru* for Universal Studios, starring Heather Graham, and formed Virgin Comics and Virgin Animation, an entertainment company focused on creating new stories and characters for a global audience, founded with Richard Branson and his Virgin Group.

'In Delhi,' Shekhar says, 'we used to sleep under the open skies on the terrace in summer. There was no light, sound or other pollution at that time. The universe was there to comprehend in all its fairytale glory. The stars were bright enough to create shadows of my hand on the white sheets. It was beautiful, as my mother would give me a glass of water from the earthen pot called the Surahi. I still miss the taste of the earth in the water I drank in the light of the universe. And as I would lie there, staring at the stars, the inevitable question would nag me again. Where does the universe go? What lies at the end of the universe . . . ?'

This is Shekhar's own prayer:

## Director's Prayer

If I am not struggling,
Is there no creative process?

If I am not exploring,
Is there no discovery?

And is it discovery I am looking for
Or is the pot of gold at the end of the rainbow
Just another deeper,
More profound,
More relevant question?

If I am not in angst with the script,
Are my characters not in angst with themselves?
Am I the director, another character in angst?
Can I live in the story?
Can I both create a world, and then step into it myself?
Who am I in this film?

The last four days have been easier.
I finished on time,
I have not been torn apart.
Is something going wrong?
Have I lost my passion?
Or am I just well prepared?
Am I too prepared?
Am I not being organic?

Please, can I continue to live on the edge?
To explore on the edge?

Please,

Let me be a sail whipped around in the wind,
Let the symphony engulf me.
And please
Can it be totally unpredictable?

And let every moment be a question
Where every thought is dispersed
And a new one rushes in to fill the vacuum.

Please do not let me become a prisoner
Of my knowledge,
Of career,
Of a job,
Of my desire
To please,
Of my need
To be appreciated.

## Cindy Kent

Cindy Kent was the first presenter to be signed up for Premier Radio in 1995, but her showbiz roots reach much deeper. She was in the profession for many years as the lead singer with The Settlers – the pop-folk group who had a hit with 'The Lightning Tree', the theme song to the TV series *Follyfoot*. They travelled the world with their special brand of music.

She developed a great love for radio and began working in the medium, starting with Radio 4, then Radio 2, and then Radio 1, which may, or may not, be progression – depending on your listening habits! She was there at the birth of commercial radio in the UK working for LBC, Radio Hallam and Capital Radio.

Cindy developed a love for training and worked with corporations, police and politicians, and even ran a course training ministers how to use a microphone, something that is so often overlooked. This led to her developing a Media Awareness Project for the Mothers' Union, taking her to Australia, Canada and many parts of the UK.

Cindy was licensed as a reader in the Church of England in 2005 and ordained as deacon in 2007, and is currently assistant curate at a North London church – as well as being kept busy at Premier Radio as the co-presenter of *Inspirational Breakfast*. Cindy has a son, James, and two cats. Her hobbies are needlework and tapestry, crosswords and Sudoku . . . and sleeping!

'My very favourite prayer – and the one I had printed on the back of my Ordination Card – is the Serenity Prayer. Most people only know the first four lines – which are lovely – but I found that there's more! Equally lovely!'

## The Serenity Prayer

God grant me the serenity
to accept the things I cannot change;
courage to change the things I can;
and wisdom to know the difference.
Living one day at a time;
Enjoying one moment at a time;
Accepting hardships as the pathway to peace;
Taking, as He did, this sinful world
as it is, not as I would have it;
Trusting that He will make all things right
if I surrender to His Will;
That I may be reasonably happy in this life
and supremely happy with Him
Forever in the next.
Amen.

Reinhold Niebuhr

# Janey Lee Grace

Janey Lee Grace is best known for being Steve Wright's co-presenter on the popular BBC Radio 2 afternoon show, as well as her own Saturday morning programme. However, she is also a very talented actress, singer and writer, and her bestselling books *Imperfectly Natural Woman* and *Imperfectly Natural Home* offer help to live life the natural way.

A regular churchgoer since her teens, Janey says, 'I went through times of disillusionment, and there were periods when I didn't set foot in church or think about it from one year to the next. But the funny thing is, I reckon it wasn't all up to me. I believe God held on to me and found ways of bringing me back into the fold.

'One aspect of faith that I do highly recommend is prayer. There have been numerous studies that suggest that people who pray are healthier and live longer. You may equate this with meditation, and of course the act of quieting your mind will reap great rewards, but prayer is slightly different in that often, but not always, it is petitionary. There is a theory that everyone prays at some point in their life, even if it's only a crisis "Lord, help me!" prayer. Incredibly, more often than not, prayers are answered, not necessarily in the way we've asked, but answered nevertheless.

'A few years ago I was going through a difficult time and I couldn't even find the words to form a prayer that might help. A spiritual counsellor I went to see showed me that in faith, as with any other aspect of life, we are all at a different stage of our journey. She helped me to find a way to use visualization as a way to talk to God and find the peace I so desired. Although I was quite disillusioned with Christianity generally, I went twice a week to St Albans cathedral and it really helped to soak up the atmosphere. When I had given my soul time to recuperate, I was ready to pray again, ready to participate, be part of a church and to offer my contribution.'

## You Know

Dear God,
You know my need; please help (as if you wouldn't; as if you haven't already) bring relief to searching; bring an end to striving; bring peace and stillness and new life. Christ, put my feet on the right path. Amen.

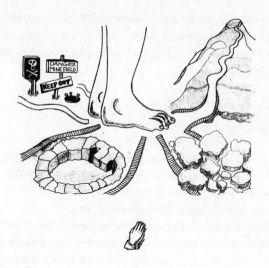

## Steve Legg

Steve Legg celebrated 21 years in showbiz in 2009 and has gained a reputation as one of the UK's top escapologists, performing in theatres and venues throughout Britain and the world.

Escapes from locked boxes, chains and handcuffs, being manacled between jeeps going in different directions, and the world-famous upside-down strait-jacket escape has taken Steve's death-defying act to over 20 countries and four continents and his numerous television appearances have been seen by millions.

In 1995 Steve was a special guest of comedy duo Tommy Cannon and Bobby Ball on their nationwide Gospel Show tour which played to packed audiences in 48 venues across the UK. A message of freedom through Christianity often runs throughout his spellbinding performances and his shows always leave young and old amused, amazed, entertained, and inspired to believe that Jesus can set them free.

In schools, colleges and universities, on the streets and in prisons, family cabaret and after-dinner entertainment, from the largest arena to the smallest TV screen, Steve's polished professionalism shines. This is his . . .

### Escapologist's Prayer

It's not the easiest thing, Lord – dangling by your ankles from some point uncomfortably high above the ground, while extricating yourself from a strait jacket.

Some might well ask, 'What's the point?'

Yet the world is full of would-be escapologists.

People tied up in knots with pressure; with stress; dangling dangerously amid relationships that have gone bad and situations they don't know how to face.

So many are desperate to escape, not just from the burdens of life – but from life itself.

Lord, as I break out of my manacles, let people see Your strength, wonder at Your power, and feel Your love for them. Show them that through You they can escape from whatever pain and trouble binds them to discover Your peace, Your joy, and Your purpose for their lives.

Help them to understand that all the freedom they need is in knowing Your Son, the one who escaped death itself – Jesus, the greatest escapologist of all time.

## Syd Little

Syd Little is one half of top comedy act Little & Large. The recipients of numerous awards for their television, club and theatre performances throughout the UK, including their own BBC TV show, which ran for 14 years, Little & Large are established as one of Britain's finest double acts and recently celebrated 48 years together.

'Most of our work from the mid-1970s became the regular round of a long summer season, followed by our TV series, followed by pantomime,' says Syd. 'We've done more than 30 pantos and there were plenty of Christmases where I felt I wasn't in control of my own life because they are always so hectic.'

It was working with Sir Cliff Richard in the 1970s that caused Syd to reconsider a childhood faith. 'I'd been a believer in my youth, but showbiz just squeezed God out,' explains Syd. 'I noticed in Cliff, and later in others like Roy Castle, that they had something I didn't.'

In 1995 Syd's eldest son Paul died of a drug overdose and his daughter had her life threatened when she was attacked by an enraged boyfriend. It brought Syd another step closer to God, but it was in Cannon & Ball's dressing room in Blackpool in 1992 that Syd finally re-committed his life to Christ.

'Christians in Entertainment had organized a Comedians' Bible Study backstage,' Syd explains. 'At first, Chris from CIE couldn't get a word in edgeways because all the comics who had come to the Bible Study were trying to tell gags. Eventually Chris got our attention and started talking about forgiveness. I knew I needed that and formally asked God back into my life then and there. It's been a fantastic journey ever since.'

God was to do more than Syd expected, when it was suggested that he tell his story in churches around the UK. Syd agreed to give it a try, and a year later he was standing on stage in a large church in Eaglescliff singing Buddy Holly songs and talking about his life, his work and his faith. Soon his 'Evening with Syd Little' in churches across the country became so successful that these days he has to put several weeks aside each year to fulfil all the requests.

'After the Hull Panto in 2001,' says Syd, 'Eddie was diagnosed with heart disease and had a complete heart transplant in 2002. With Eddie out of action, I suddenly realized that I was out of a job! Fortunately, because I had the experience of doing solo gospel gigs I had the confidence to try out my performance in commercial situations too. God must have seen this coming, which is why he got me prepared all those years before. Now I knew that although the future seemed bleak, he was somehow going to look after me.

'I have always been a churchgoer and believed in God, but it never had much to do with the reality of my life, and all the difficulties I faced. Now I know that whatever happens, God is with me, and helps me through.'

There has been a public fascination with Syd's life. As well as his autobiography, *Little by Little*, his laughter book, *A Little Heavenly Humour*, remains a bestseller and his new DVD life story caused much attention in the press and media.

'I'm glad that within all the madness of showbiz I have managed to keep my feet on the ground and keep doing the decorating and pulling my family around me,' Syd adds. 'I've always been me. I've enjoyed every moment as special. I have never regretted anything I have done in my life. Now I realize I am being guided, and whatever happens this will see me through.

'One of the songs I have recently used to finish my gospel gigs is the one made famous by Daniel O'Donnell. It's based on the famous "Footsteps" poem where a man questions God about the fact that there are two sets of footprints in the sand, apart from the really bad times when there was just one set.

'"Why did you leave me when I needed you most?" questions the man.

'God explains that it was when the man needed him most that this was when God was carrying him. The single set of footprints in the sand were God's.

'So I often sing this song because it sums up my spiritual life and experience so well.'

## Footsteps

Footsteps walking with me
Footsteps I cannot see
But every move I make
And every step I take
I know they're there with me
They walk with me all the way
Beside me day by day
Through good and bad
Through happy and sad
Those footsteps won't go away

I'll never walk in life alone
There'll always be someone there
I know he won't let me down
He's with me everywhere
The special things in life I've done
Have been through him and his love
I've been blessed in so many ways
Thanks to the Lord above

Footsteps walking with me
Footsteps I cannot see
But every move I make
And every step I take

I know they're there with me
They walk with me all the way
Beside me day by day
Through good and bad
Through happy and sad
Those footsteps won't go away

I think that my life's been planned
By the one who's guiding me
When I'm led by the hand
Of someone I can't see
I'm not always sure where to go
That's when I follow his lead
I know that the pathway that he shows
Will help me to succeed

Footsteps walking with me
Footsteps I cannot see
But every move I make
And every step I take
I know they're there with me
They walk with me all the way
Beside me day by day
Through good and bad
Through happy and sad
By my side they will stay

Author unknown

Syd credits the ability to get through all the ups and downs of his life to his faith, family, friends and the gift of humour, something he is keen to reflect in these two prayers he has chosen about getting older . . .

## The Senility Prayer

God grant me the senility to forget the people
I never liked anyway,
the good fortune to run into the ones that I do,
and the eyesight to tell the difference.

Now that I'm older, I thank you that I've discovered that:

ONE
I started out with nothing, and I still have most of it.

TWO
I finally got my head together; now my body is falling apart.

THREE
Funny, I don't remember being absent-minded . . .

FOUR
It is easier to get older than it is to get wiser.

FIVE
It's hard to make a comeback when you haven't been
anywhere.

SIX
The only time the world beats a path to your door is when
you're in the bathroom.

SEVEN
If God wanted me to touch my toes, he would have put them
on my knees.

EIGHT
When I'm finally holding all the cards, why does everyone
decide to play chess?

NINE
It's not hard to meet expenses . . . they're everywhere.

TEN
These days, I spend a lot of time thinking about the hereafter
. . . I go somewhere to get something and then wonder what
I'm here after. Amen.

Author unknown

## The Gift of Being Older

Dear Lord,
I am now, probably for the first time in my life, the person
I have always wanted to be. Oh, not my body! I sometimes
despair over my body, the wrinkles, the baggy eyes, and my
sagging bottom. Often I am taken aback by that old person
that lives in my mirror, but I don't agonize over those things
for long.

I would never trade my amazing friends, my wonderful life
or my loving family for less grey hair or a flatter belly. As I've
aged, I've become more kind to myself, and less critical of
myself. I've become my own friend. I don't chide myself for
eating that extra biscuit, or for not making my bed, or for
buying that silly cement gnome that I didn't need, but looks
so avant-garde on my patio. I am entitled to a treat, to be
messy, to be extravagant.

I have seen too many dear friends leave this world too soon; before they understood the great freedom that comes with ageing. Whose business is it if I choose to read or play on the computer until 4 a.m. and sleep until noon?

I will dance with myself to those wonderful tunes of the '60s and '70s, and if I, at the same time, wish to weep over a lost love . . . I will.

I will walk the beach in a swimsuit that is stretched over a bulging body, and will dive into the waves with abandon if I choose to, despite the pitying glances from the jet set. They, too, will get old.

I know I am sometimes forgetful. But there again, some of life is just as well forgotten. And I eventually remember the important things.

Sure, over the years my heart has been broken. How can your heart not break when you lose a loved one, or when a child suffers, or even when somebody's beloved pet gets hit by a car? But broken hearts are what give us strength and understanding and compassion. A heart never broken is pristine and sterile and will never know the joy of being imperfect.

I am so blessed to have lived long enough to have my hair turning grey, and to have my youthful laughs forever etched into deep grooves on my face. So many have never laughed, and so many have died before their hair could turn silver.

As I get older, it is easier to be positive. I care less about what other people think. I don't question myself any more. I've even earned the right to be wrong.

So, Lord, I like being old. It has set me free. I like the person I have become. I am not going to live for ever, but while I am still here, I will not waste time lamenting what could have been, or worrying about what will be. And I shall eat dessert every single day (if I feel like it). Amen.

Author unknown

# Shane Lynch

Shane Lynch is a member of the Irish band Boyzone, one of the most successful boy bands of all time. In recent years he has excelled in motor sports and has taken part in a number of reality television shows including *The Games*, *Love Island* and, most recently, *Cirque de Celebrité*.

Kicked out of school at the age of 14, Shane had no grand plan or burning ambitions. He just took life as it came, surviving on his boyish charm and gift of the blag. So when a friend asked him how he felt about forming a boy band he thought, 'Sure, why not?' He didn't sing, he didn't play an instrument, but, hey, so what? He'd make it up as he went along. He was a survivor.

When the Boyzone phenomenon finally took off, Shane soon started to kick against the manic world he found himself hurled into. Relentless media pressure, a dangerous foray into the occult, his marriage breakdown, and the eventual band break-up took their toll on a man who could never quite get to grips with what all the fuss was about.

The fame game is not all it's cracked up to be, as Shane explains: 'I'd once been an ordinary, rational human being but, bit by bit, I was changed into a thoroughly nasty piece of work, a hopeless, evil man. Anger churned around inside me almost all the time and I was weighed down under the influence of the things I had been messing around with. A lot of the time I thought I'd fallen into hell. There was nothing but blackness. I knew I was in deep trouble.'

Shane had already experimented with a home-made ouija board when he was just 14. It spelt out 'Kill Shane', and left him shocked and terrified, and opened the door to many other unwelcome and frightening supernatural visitations. 'Once I was staying in a hotel in Germany. I was in a very deep sleep when I was woken by the sound of footsteps padding across my room. They came up right behind me and I sensed someone or something leaning over me. I could hear breathing. I was so scared I couldn't move or shout or scream. I remember the sound of the breathing stopping and the footsteps retreating and I'd never been so frightened in my whole life.'

Searches for answers via mediums couldn't break the demonic influence that Shane seemed to be under, but a Christian singer called Ben Ofoedu helped him find the peace he was seeking by saying that it was possible to find real freedom through a personal relationship with God. Shane had achieved fame and fortune beyond his wildest dreams – and ended up angry, disillusioned, empty and alone. Then when Ben told Shane about God, little by little, his new faith helped him put the shattered pieces of his life back together.

Boyzone's recent UK tour saw 200,000 tickets selling out within two hours, and Shane's autobiography, *The Chancer*, continues to sell well. As Shane says, 'Since handing my life over to God, I know that whatever happens, the future is in God's hands. It's no good looking to my hopes and dreams because I've learned that God always has something much, much better.'

## Prayer of Charles de Foucauld

Father,
I abandon myself into your hands;
do with me what you will.
Whatever you may do, I thank you:
I am ready for all, I accept all.
Let only your will be done in me
and in all your creatures.
I wish no more than this, O Lord.
Into your hands I commend my soul:
I offer it to you
with all the love of my heart,
for I love you, Lord,
and so need to give myself,
to surrender myself into your hands
without reserve,
and with boundless confidence,
for you are my Father.

# Don Maclean

Don Maclean presented BBC Radio 2's religious flagship programme *Good Morning Sunday* for many years; it may have seemed glamorous, but having to get up in the early hours of Sunday morning to get to the studio brings it all back down to earth. It's particularly hard when you've only just slumped into bed at 2 a.m. the night before.

'At least on radio they can't see the bags under your eyes,' smiles Don. Don is very much at ease in any situation that he finds himself in, and attributes much of this to his deep faith. He is concerned to be fully professional, but fully Christian too. He says it's not always easy to achieve both at the same time, but he tries!

Don is one of the UK's leading television and cabaret performers. He first came to the public's attention through his appearances on the BBC's *Black and White Minstrel Show*, which he hosted for three years on television and five years on stage. He has starred in six Royal Command performances and appeared in over 30 pantomimes, several of which he wrote and directed.

His enjoyment of squash culminates with him having won the British Celebrity Championships two years running. Don is also an experienced pilot, and regularly flies his own aircraft. He is proud of the fact that despite being surrounded by many showbiz marriages that seem to fail, he has been married to his wife, Toni, for 30 years.

'If I'm asked to sum up what being a Christian means to me, I say it's about never being afraid,' he says. 'We live in a world that sometimes seems intent on scaring us. We can purchase an insurance policy for almost any eventuality these days, and even have insurance policies to protect claims on our insurance policies!

'We have all been enveloped by fear at one time or another, and this has the effect of making us a prisoner. The little boy, who is afraid of the dark, is too scared to go out of his room at night, so he stays where he is. Fear can cause us to freeze up and stop us doing what we want to do.

'I know that God is always on the lookout for me, and if I pray in times of strife or danger he will be right there for me. My faith in God's ability to protect me, and the opportunity to bring my fears before him in prayer, are the key antidotes to fear.

'What are you afraid of? Rejection, sickness, uncertainty or death? We can't overcome fear just by ignoring it. But we can overcome our fears with God's help; as we hand over our fears to him, we will sense that the "light of his salvation" can extinguish the darkness of fear.'

## Uncluttered Faith

Dear God,
Thank you for the gift of faith.
Faith to know that I can trust you to uphold me when I feel fear trying to overwhelm me.
Lord, please give me the faith I had as a small child, faith that is uncluttered and simply enables me to believe in you and all your works. Amen.

## Cat's Prayer

Now I lay me down to sleep
I pray this cushy life to keep

I pray for toys that look like mice
and warm cushions soft and nice

For grocery bags where I can hide
Just like a tiger crouched inside

I pray for gourmet kitty snacks
and someone nice to scratch my back

For window sills all warm and bright
for shadows to explore by night

I pray I'll always stay real cool
and keep the secret feline rule

To never tell a human that
The world is really run by cats.

Author unknown

## Katherine Mansi

Katherine Mansi says, 'I believe I was born to dance. It's been a lifetime passion of mine as long as I can remember. My mother says I entered the world with both feet doing high kicks and I haven't stopped since!'

Indeed, Katherine follows a family line of professional performers: 'My mum and dad met while working together on the late '60s West End hit, *Phil the Fluter*, at the Palace Theatre, with Stanley Baxter. Mum had danced around the world with the English National Ballet and Dad enjoyed numerous London shows and tours, so I suppose it was a profession I was bound to adopt.'

Katherine studied at the Bush Davies School and at the Doreen Bird College of Performing Arts, and since then has appeared in many musicals, variety shows and pantomimes, including playing the title roles in *Aladdin* and *Dick Whittington*. She is principal of her own popular theatre dance school in Kent, and has been teaching children and adults for the last 20 years.

Katherine works as choreographer for numerous professional musicals, variety shows and pantomimes, including national tours and long summer seasons. She most especially enjoyed working on perhaps the glitziest production in the country, *Bobby Crush's Liberace – Live from Las Vegas!*

'I love the opportunity to wear all manner of costumes, but a showgirl outfit must be one of the nicest,' Katherine says. 'All wrapped up in feathers and sequins, the dancers feel a million dollars on stage and can confidently strut their stuff for an appreciative audience. Many shows are working on tight budgets these days, so it's always a privilege to work with producers who see costumes as an important part of the entertainment and complementary to the dance.'

For many, uninhibited dancing is one of the most pleasurable exercises around and can distract even the most committed worrier, so no wonder it's seen as a divine gift.

'I love the bits in the Bible that talk about dancing, including Jeremiah with God's promise that there will be a day when we will "go out to dance with the joyful" and "maidens will dance and be glad",' says Katherine. 'I think there will be plenty of dancing when we get to heaven, and I can't wait! Till then, I will just try to use this wonderful gift in the best way that I can, and my prayer expresses sincere thanks to the creator for providing it to all of us.'

## Dancer's Prayer

Thank you, God,
For those who have been given the gift
Of the joy of movement and dance.
The ultimate freedom.
To express oneself through movement is exhilarating.
To become totally absorbed by the flow of steps,
And the music from within.
It is a divine gift.

Given because you love us
And you want us to experience life in all its fullness.
Thank you.

## A Prayer of William Penn

Lord,
Help me not to despise or oppose
What I do not understand.

# Allen Mechen

Allen Mechen never thought much about God when he was young: 'I only knew about the characters from Bible stories told to us at school, and where I lived in the North East if you went to church and talked about Jesus, you were seen as different to everybody else. I always liked the stories from the Bible, though; they used to make me feel good. As a boy, I remember going to the pictures to see *The Ten Commandments* with Charlton Heston playing the part of Moses. I thought it was amazing, and I came out of the cinema feeling inspired. Maybe I could achieve something great in my life too, just as he did? Even though I was a pretty cocky, confident young lad, I didn't think it was possible to see the Red Sea part, but at least I had my music and I loved playing guitar. Perhaps God could use this in my life?!

'God didn't feature much in my thoughts over the next few years, but when I was 21 I was rushed into hospital and diagnosed with tuberculosis. It was a rare and serious disease. My lung had collapsed, and I had to have an immediate operation as my life was suddenly at risk. The ward was full of old people, and two of them died while I was there. I thought, "Well, this is it! I'm going to die . . .", and so I prayed that God wouldn't let me go. "I'm too young," I implored with him.

'I don't know what it was, but something changed in me, and after a long 18 months battling with the infection whose grip was so hard to shift from my body, I was well again and went back to work. My answered prayer gave me a feeling of being rescued, and ever since then I felt that God was great, and it was the start of a very long on-and-off journey to discover more about him.

'I was fortunate enough to have a long career in the music and comedy business and enjoyed good acting parts in films and television series such as *Brookside*, *Byker Grove* and *Auf Wiedersehen Pet*, as well as being the familiar face on a very famous packet of crisps for many years!

'After decades of TV appearances and playing in rock and comedy bands, my wife Margaret and I moved abroad to the island of Lanzarote, where I worked in the nightclubs for ten years while enjoying the constant sunshine. Interestingly enough, God followed me out there too, and this is where we both gave our hearts to God after finding out that our neighbours were Christians.

'They introduced us to the International Evangelical Church where we discovered that Christians don't have to be boring or churches irrelevant. In fact, when I became part of the live band in church, I found that it can be exciting to be a Christian, using the gifts and talents the Lord had blessed me with, playing guitar and singing. I realized then that God has a plan for us all. This is a prayer I wrote to remind me where talents such as music come from.'

## God, You Are Amazing

I just want to thank you, Lord, for all the gifts and blessings you pour on us every day.

I would especially like to thank you, Lord, for the talent you gave me, this musical gift of being able to play the guitar and sing.

I believe that our talents are God-given, and that none of this would be possible without the opportunities to use those skills that you have given us.

Lord, music is the spice of life, and there is no better way for me to spread your precious word than through music. Thank you, dear Lord.

'When Margaret and I recently moved back to the UK,' Allen explains, 'I had no idea where the work would come from as all my ties with agents and bookers had been severed and the whole entertainment scene had changed dramatically. A prayer for help was on my lips when we decided to try out a local church for the first time. Amazingly, after the service, I was introduced to a professional theatre producer who was also visiting that day. When we got talking he said he had been looking for someone to play the part of Alderman Fitzwarren in his new pantomime production of *Dick Whittington* and he virtually booked me then and there! God is great.

'I know now from personal experience that God plays a big part in my life, blessing me with many talents, opportunities and divine appointments, and I know that he will continue to open doors for me as I rebuild my career back in the UK. This is a song I wrote that best expresses how I feel about the one who has taken such a caring interest in all that I have done over the years.'

## I Love You, Sweet Jesus

You know I'll never forsake you my Lord
you know I never would
You're with me every day of my life
And you always make me feel so good
Yes you always make me feel so good

There are times when I feel so alone
No one ever should
Then I remember everything that you taught me
Your living word flows in my blood
Yes your living word just flows in my blood

CHORUS
I love you sweet Jesus
I love you my Lord
I know that you're with me now
And you protect me with your shield and your sword
Yes you protect me with your shield and your sword

I give you all the glory my Lord
You know it's true
I will praise you all the days of my life
Through the darkness your light will shine through
Yes through the darkness your light will shine through

I can't wait to see you face to face
You know it's true
If I have to wait the rest of my life
I will always be faithful and true
Knowing one day that I'll be there with you

Eternity is such a long, long time
You know it's true

I'll be happy all the rest of my days
Knowing one day that I'll be there with you
Face to face in heaven with you
Knowing one day that I'll be there it's true
Face to face in heaven with you
Face to face in heaven with you
Amen.

Our lager, which art in barrels, Hallowed be thy drink. Thy will be drunk, I will be drunk, At home as it is in the tavern. Give us this day our foamy head, And forgive us our spillages, As we forgive those who spill against us. And lead us not to incarceration, But deliver us from hangovers. For thine is the beer, the bitter, the lager. Ramen.

## Lloyd Notice

Lloyd Notice enjoyed playing the part of Mufasa in Disney's *The Lion King* in London's West End, but found that the part was quite physically demanding: 'Every night I had to fall off a cliff top while being suspended by safety wires. Eventually, like a lot of the other actors before me, it damaged my back and I had to have a course of physiotherapy to get me back to normal.

'The make-up was very specific and was based on the vibrant tribal colours of Africa and would take about an hour for the make-up artist to apply. As I sat there while all the different layers were applied, I found it was a good time to prepare for my nightly performance, and a good time to pray.

'The story is centred on the young lion, Simba, who learns all about love and responsibility, and I think that is a great theme for the church today, love but with responsibility. My prayer is always . . . as follows.'

## Reaching Others

Father God,
Please touch people through our performance
Whether we mention our faith or not,
So that many will come to know the real you. Amen.

'It's a sad fact for an actor that so many are out of work at any one time, and employment is often searched for on a regular basis. Rejection at auditions is not uncommon, but it's another good opportunity to be able to throw these worries heavenwards . . .'

## Prayer for Employment

God, our Father,
I turn to you, seeking your divine help and guidance
as I look for suitable employment.
I need your wisdom to guide my footsteps along the right
    path,
and to lead me to find the proper things to say
and do in this quest.
I wish to use the gifts and talents you have given me,
but I need the opportunity to do so with gainful employment.

Do not abandon me, dear Father, in this search,
but rather grant me this favour I seek
so that I may return to you with praise and thanksgiving
for your gracious assistance.
Grant this through Christ, our Lord. Amen.

Author unknown

## A Dog's Prayer

Treat me kindly, my beloved master, for no heart in all
the world is more grateful for kindness than the loving
heart of me.

Do not break my spirit with a stick, for though I should
lick your hand between the blows, your patience and
understanding will more quickly teach me the things you
would have me do.

Speak to me often, for your voice is the world's sweetest
music, as you must know by the fierce wagging of my
tail when your footstep falls upon my waiting ear.

When it is cold and wet, please take me inside, for I am
now a domesticated animal, no longer used to the bitter
elements. And I ask no greater glory than the privilege
of sitting at your feet beside the hearth. Though had you
no home, I would rather follow through ice and snow
than rest upon the softest pillow in the warmest home in
all the land, for you are my god and I am your devoted
worshipper.

Keep my dish filled with fresh water, for although I should not reproach you were it dry, I cannot tell you when I suffer thirst. Feed me clean food, that I may stay well, to romp and play and do your bidding, to walk by your side, and stand ready, willing and able to protect you with my life should your life be in danger.

And, beloved master, should the great Master see fit to deprive me of my health or sight, do not turn me away from you. Rather hold me gently in your arms as skilled hands grant me the merciful boon of eternal rest – and I will leave you knowing with the last breath I drew, my fate was ever safest in your hands. Amen.

Author unknown

## Simeon Oakes

Simeon Oakes is about to be launched into one of the most strange, unpredictable and wild businesses there is ... showbusiness!

'Well ... my story certainly isn't as exciting as any of the others in this book,' Simeon says, 'but perhaps that's because I'm at the very start of my career?

'I graduated from the University of Kent in the summer of 2007 with a BA in Drama & English and American literature, with first-class honours. Since then, I've been working in Mont Tauch, my local winery, as an export sales assistant, trying to earn enough money to go to drama school. I'm currently auditioning at DSL, LAMDA, RADA and Mountview – hopefully, for a start in six to twelve months' time.

'My family moved to Paziols in the South of France in 1989 when I was almost four, and planted a church that is still going strong. I did all my education there up to the equivalent of A levels, then went back to the UK for university. I'm now in my early twenties.

'I've always had a passion for acting and took part in as many performances and plays as I could. It was at university that, boosted by my experience there as well as the influence of my entourage, I decided I wanted to try my very best to achieve my goal. Since then, I've only had one idea in mind: going for it, and giving it a shot. I have nothing to lose. If I succeed I've fulfilled a dream, and if I don't try, I know I'll always regret it!

'In five years, my ideal plan would be to have been propelled into the industry after drama school and to have been involved in a number of plays in respected theatres. I'd also be auditioning and perhaps already be getting parts in films. Of course, that's in an ideal world, and I'm fully aware it is quite possible that that will not necessarily be the case. My ideal has always been to start in the theatre, my "first love", and then to evolve into acting on screen while still being on stage.

'My passion and desire for cinema and film was reinforced in December 2008 when I had the fantastic opportunity to be an extra in Justin Chadwick's screen adaptation of *The Other Boleyn Girl* with Natalie Portman, Scarlett Johansson, Eric Bana and Kristin Scott Thomas. It was the most amazing and exciting experience. I took part in two major scenes: the beheading of Anne Boleyn and George Boleyn, both as a peasant and a nobleman. If you look very carefully, know where and when to look and don't blink, you might just catch a glimpse of me! It really was a thrilling experience. Seeing Natalie Portman performing the same scene over and over again, with the same intensity every single time, was amazing.

'So, perhaps as I pass through drama school and all the hurdles of getting in, up and on in this strange business, and with God guiding me every step of the way, it will become as exciting as all the other stories in this book.

'Here's my own prayer for all those who are facing auditions, job interviews and every kind of similar hurdle . . .'

## Audition Prayer

Dear Lord . . .

I'm trembling all over, Lord! My legs won't stop shaking, Lord!

And my feet . . .! Well, they just won't stand in one place, Lord!

I feel like war is raging inside my stomach, Lord.

There are so many others here, Lord, and they all want the same as I do, Lord!

They all look so much more experienced and prepared and better looking and . . . well . . . relaxed, Lord!

I think I don't want to be here right now, Lord.

But . . . I've been dreaming of this moment for years, Lord.

I know there's nowhere else I'd rather be . . . Lord!

O Lord, why do I keep saying 'Lord'?

And why am I telling you all this anyway?

You know my heart, Lord, you know my soul!

You know that I'm here because I'm fulfilling my dream, the desire of my heart,

The desire you yourself placed inside me, even before I had a heart!

That's why I'm telling you this, Lord, because you delight in hearing it, and in hearing me calling you 'Lord'!

Because you told me that to receive, all I needed to do was ask!

So, Lord, I ask, O Lord, I pray,

That you would take the fear away (although, the feeling is
   not so unpleasant in a funny kind of way)
That you would hold my hand as I enter, and never let me go!
O Lord, help me to tell them, help me to show them how I
   feel,
Help me to express as truly as is humanly possible, that you
   created me for this.
Prince of peace, let it all be in your hands.
The fears, the joy, the excitement . . . the disappointment.
Let your will be done in me and through me.
Jesus, in your precious name I pray . . .
Oh, and Lord . . . please don't let me forget my lines . . .
   again . . .
. . . Lord!

## Teenager's Prayer

With each new day that dawns I am growing up,
   O Lord.
It's not too soon to start thinking of what I want to be.
It's very hard, I think,
to make the right decision
but I pray that you will help and guide me.
Show me what to do,
let me share, someday,
my talents where they're needed.
And when you show me,
give me courage to be generous enough
to do what you want. Amen.

Author unknown

# Danny Owen

Danny Owen has been a top international vocal impressionist since leaving school. He has worked all over the world in cabaret, on television, radio, stage and films, and is one of the most experienced and professional performers on the tribute circuit today.

In 1996 he appeared on Granada TV's *Stars in their Eyes* as Julio Iglesias. He received incredible praise from the media for his performance. With this kind of exposure, Danny decided to put together a sensational tribute show of the Spanish heartthrob, singing in both English and Spanish. His portrayal was recognized as being so accurate that it immediately got him an appearance in San Juan, Puerto Rico, at the El Conquistador Resort Hotel, for a multi-billionaire American client. From there he was contracted for six months to appear at Bally's Hilton in Atlantic City, New Jersey, and went on to appear at the Luxor and Imperial Palace hotels in Las Vegas.

Danny's Christian faith means that he can celebrate the gift of music whenever and wherever he performs. He says, 'My prayer is the simplest one I know and I've used it many, many times . . .'

## Help!

Dear God, help!

## Sarum Prayer

God be in my head
and in my understanding.
God be in my eyes
and in my looking.
God be in my mouth
and in my speaking.
God be in my heart
and in my thinking.
God be at my end
and at my departing.

*Sarum Book of Hours*, 1514

# James Owen

James Owen is known as the man with the golden voice, and has an infectious personality and a zany sense of humour. He recently toured the UK with *Palladium Memories*, playing his comedy heroes Harry Secombe, Benny Hill and Terry Scott. He enthrals audiences around the country with his one-man shows and, as well as working alongside many of the UK's best-known names, is just as at home performing in cabaret and residential homes. This is his prayer:

## Aren't People Funny, Lord?

Dear Lord,

Thanks for all your help in keeping me safe from the germs and bugs I meet every day as I sing to the elderly in homes up and down the country, especially those times when I've been sneezed over and dribbled on.

Sometimes I feel uplifted in my spirit when I get a good reception and they sing along and laugh at my jokes, but sometimes I feel low when it might have been more exciting to sing in the local cemetery.

Aren't people funny, Lord? I mean, why is it that as we get older we seem to lose all the inhibitions we once held dear? Some of the unkind comments I get really hurt me, Lord, although I hope I never let it show. Comments about my portly size are often hard to cope with, such as these ones that I heard recently right in the middle of my song: 'Are you likely to get any fatter? Because if you are we shall have to get the doors widened!' Or, 'If you chopped his legs 'orf he'd roll around for ever!' They think they're being funny, but they still hurt, Lord, so please help me to cope with them.

Anyway, I need to get ready for another show, so let's you and me together, Lord, prepare to face the dribblers who were born earlier. I know that you love them, Lord, they are your children just as I am. So help me keep my spirits up, my voice sweet, my health clean, and my sanity intact. Amen.

A little girl, dressed in her Sunday best, was running as fast as she could, trying not to be late for Bible class. As she ran she prayed, 'Dear Lord, please don't let me be late! Dear Lord, please don't let me be late!'

As she was running and praying, she tripped on a curb and fell, getting her clothes dirty and tearing her dress. She got up, brushed herself off, and started running again. As she ran she once again began to pray, 'Dear Lord, please don't let me be late! . . . But don't shove me either!'

## Nick Page

Nick Page opened his innings in Doncaster in 1943, thereby qualifying himself by geography, if little else, to play cricket for Yorkshire. At school, at Dulwich, he blamed his total inability to shine at any sport (and his premature middle-aged spread) on the results of polio, which had kept him in Guy's Hospital for three months when he was seven years old.

An early overture to the BBC (for the post of Light Programme announcer!) was not positively received, so after an abortive year at medical school, he did a four-year course in business administration, ending up in the import–export business selling waxes and vanilla beans.

In 1970 he became manager of Hildenborough Hall, a Christian conference centre. While there he began contributing to programmes on the local BBC station, Radio Medway (now Radio Kent).

In 1975 he went freelance, taking over responsibility for the religious programmes on London's first commercial radio station (LBC) and at the same time becoming a regular presenter of the nightly four-hour phone-in show, *Nightline*.

Soon he was presenting children's programmes for BBC Radio 4; and also on Radio 2, introducing orchestral programmes and developing his own show on Sunday mornings.

During the run of the *Nick Page Programme* he presented a number of outside broadcasts, including ones from Iona, Jerusalem, Rome, Los Angeles, and just south of the equator, from Kisumu in Kenya.

He interviewed people as varied as Mother Teresa, Margaret Thatcher, Diana Dors, Pat Boone, Billy Graham, Malcolm Muggeridge and Cardinal Basil Hume.

He then spent eight years as announcer/newsreader on BBC Radio 2.

In the mid-1990s Nick was in at the beginning of the London station, Premier Radio, presenting several programmes – and producing an entertaining knock-out quiz between churches in the region. This period included the 1997 General Election campaign during which he hosted a nightly *Hustings* programme, where studio guests included parliamentarians from both front-benches.

The powers-that-be have decided that Nick sounds better than he looks so his television experience has been fleeting: presenting a regional news magazine, film and theatre reviewing, interviewing, announcing for a couple of now defunct ITV stations, and presenting two editions of *Songs of Praise*. He was also the London area organizer for the attempt to launch the Christian Cable Channel ARK2.

Away from broadcasting he has produced conferences and public events throughout the UK and around the world, from Budapest to Barcelona, Kuala Lumpur to Istanbul. He was also responsible for the development of the All Souls Orchestra's 'Prom Praise' concerts in London, around the UK, and beyond.

Nick is now chairman of Christians in Entertainment,

trustee of the International Christian Media Commission, and of FEBA Radio, and an ambassador for SAT-7 Television.

Arising from his involvement in Christians in Entertainment, Nick links a number of celebrities who are happy to speak about their faith with churches who are planning special outreach events.

He is a member of St James Church, Clerkenwell, where he supports the home groups and leads the drama team.

## Help Me, Lord

Loving heavenly Father,

Help me to worship you, both in my words as I pray to you, and in my life as I try to live every day in your presence.

Help me to rest in you, confident that you know me better than I know myself, and that you have my best interests at heart.

Help me to show something of your character to others, as the Holy Spirit grows your fruit in my life – love, joy, peace, patience, kindness, goodness, faithfulness, gentleness and self-control.

Help me to serve you wherever you put me; to use my hands to help those in need, and my voice to communicate your truth.

In Jesus' name,
Amen.

## Open My Eyes and My Ears

Lord Jesus,
I ask you to open my eyes
as you did with the blind man,
so that I may really see.
Tune my ears
as you did with the man who was deaf and dumb,
so that I may really hear
what you are saying to me.
May the many experiences of my senses
remind me to be aware of others
and of all that is around me.
May all that I experience
lead me closer to you.

Author unknown

# Lance Pierson

Lance Pierson is an actor who understands what it means to bring words to life. He has created many humorous and moving entertainments for a wide variety of audiences from churches to literary festivals, and as an alternative for groups who usually have speakers. He performs Bible passages, the work of poets from William Shakespeare to John Betjeman, sketches from music hall, and even the literature of cricket.

In the last ten years Lance has taken his Christian and secular presentations all around the UK. He has performed Bible passages on the main stage of the Keswick convention, Spring Harvest and Easter People. He has taken his shows

'The 90 Minute Bible' and 'Mark's Gospel' to churches of all denominations. He believes that we have a powerful resource in God's word and that so often we lose all of its power because it is read in a routine manner.

Lance has also created biographical one-man shows about some of the great English poets (John Betjeman, Gerard Manley Hopkins, John Milton, George Herbert and William Cowper), who were all Christians too. Lance has performed their poems at the Victoria and Albert Museum, Westminster Abbey, the Edinburgh Festival Fringe and literary festivals everywhere in between.

Lance prays this text prayer before every performance:

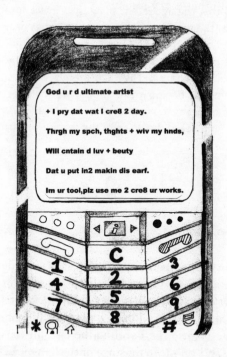

Lance says, 'I find the following passage from the flautist Sir James Galway's autobiography especially inspiring for prayer, and I'm grateful to him for allowing me to reproduce it here. Galway had broken his arms and legs in a bad accident before he wrote this.'

### Being the Best

I decided that henceforward I would play every concert, cut every record, give every TV performance, as though it were my last. I've come to understand that it is never possible to guess what might happen next; that the roof might fall in any time and that the important thing is to make sure that every time I play the flute my performance will be as near perfection and full of true music as God intended, and that I shall not be remembered for a shoddy performance. My ambitions, therefore, are limited. They are merely that I should leave good memories behind me; that people should feel when they recall my name, that in some odd, inexplicable way, they have at some time heard the voice of the infinite through me.

James Galway

## Andrea Poyser

Andrea Poyser's career began at the very early age of seven in the role of Molly in the West End production of *Annie*. She then went on to train at the Guildford School of Acting on the musical theatre course, graduating in 1992. Her first major shows were as lead vocalist in the national tour of the *Black and White Minstrels*, the comedy part of Myrtle in *Jack and the Beanstalk*, a rep season in Yeovil and Worthing playing Hilaret in *Lock Up Your Daughters*, Jean in *Having a Ball*, Betty in *Dangerous Corner*, Princess Marigold in *Jack and the Beanstalk* at the Thameside Theatre, and Maisie in the musical *The Boy Friend* at the Farnborough Theatre.

Andrea spent a summer season in Jersey as lead vocalist in the *Songs from Broadway*, and other musical work includes Mrs Potiphar in the tour of *Joseph and the Amazing Technicolor Dreamcoat*, a rep season as Audrey in the *Little Shop of Horrors* UK Tour, Sonia in the tour of *Godspell*, and Angie in the musical *Viva Ibiza* at the Millfield Theatre, which then toured to Lincoln Theatre. After playing Beverley in *Abigail's Party* at the Millfield Theatre, Andrea then went off to be lead vocalist on the P&O cruise ship the *Oriana*.

Andrea has also worked on the ship *Disney Wonder*, playing the fairy godmother in the musical *Disney Dreams* and Pain in the musical *Hercules*. Also, she has just graduated with a BA honours degree in Theatre Studies which has taken her four years to complete. In her home town of Burnham-on-Crouch, Andrea runs a community drama school for local children, with over 150 youngsters attending. As well as directing productions, she runs her own theatre company, Dramatheatrerama, writing and directing TIE productions for local councils. The latest production to have toured was the musical *Bully*, which was seen by 3,000 children. She has written various plays on antisocial behaviour, drugs and alcohol, and has taught drama to adults with special needs. Andrea's latest project is a comedy sitcom which she is currently writing. She has recently finished touring in the hit comedy play *Mum's the Word*.

Amid this challenging lifestyle, Andrea has a little boy called Laughlin, aged two, and also a very supportive husband who works in Children's Services.

Andrea says, 'My faith and the unity of my family work with me in everything I do and I'm blessed to be able to project this in my teaching, acting, and love for the theatre. And it's a true blessing to be able to perform on stage.

'I've chosen this prayer as it is so earthy and "real" – like my own words when speaking to God. And it's quite profound in that it is very fitting in my own reflectiveness of life.'

## Help Me Relax

Lord, help me to relax about insignificant details beginning tomorrow at 11.41.23 a.m.

God, help me to consider people's feelings, even if most of them ARE hypersensitive.

God, help me to take responsibility for my own actions, even though they're usually NOT my fault.

God, help me not try to RUN everything. But, if you need some help, just ask.

Lord, help me to be more laid back and help me to do it EXACTLY right.

Lord, help me to stand up for my rights (if you don't mind my asking).

God, help me to take things more seriously, especially parties and dancing.

God, give me patience, and I mean right NOW.

Lord, help me not to be a perfectionist. (Did I spell that correctly?)

God, help me to finish everything I sta . . .

God, help me to keep my mind on one thing at a time.

God, help me to do only what I can and trust you for the rest. Do you mind putting that in writing?

Lord, keep me open to others' ideas, WRONG though they may be.

Lord, help me be less independent, but let me do it my way.
Lord, help me follow established procedures today. On
  second thoughts, I'll settle for a few minutes.
Lord, help me slow downandnotrushthroughwhatIdo.
  Amen.

Author unknown

Dear Lord, please, Lord, keep your arm around my
shoulder and your hand over my mouth. Amen.

## Sir Cliff Richard

Sir Cliff Richard survived flower-power, metal, glam rock,
junk, the punk, disco, technical bods, computer music –
anything, you name it. So said the late Mickie Most on the
career of one of the UK's most enduring pop stars – Cliff
Richard. Indeed, Cliff seems to have crossed all the musical boundaries and fashions over the years, and in fact has
had a record in the charts for the equivalent of over 25
years!

Having worked extremely hard in the business for so
long, it is an earned luxury for Cliff that he can now choose
how to spend most of his time.

He has never been shy about his faith, but he's never been
one to force it down other people's throats either. When
asked, he talks happily about the day he became very aware
that Jesus was not just some myth or legend, but a living
reality. Although it took a lot of courage to stand up and tell

the world that he was a Christian, the journey to that point was a lot more private and lengthy.

Finding himself locked in religious arguments with colleagues in dressing rooms around the world on a regular basis, Cliff knew that he was eager to find some answers. He was rich and famous, but somehow did not feel fulfilled, and wanted something more than showbusiness could offer him. Christianity seemed to have been an obvious place to start, but he suddenly realized that he actually knew very little about it.

The answers eventually came through Christian friends who knew him, and before long he was attending Bible classes and, occasionally, church. Amazingly, this steady journey to faith was kept from the press, until on 16 June 1966 Cliff stood up in Earls Court at the Billy Graham Crusade meeting and simply said, 'I'm a Christian.'

The news headlined the world's papers the next day. No one in the music business or in the entertainment world had ever made such a public declaration of something so personal. Not all the press were kind-hearted about the news. Some suggested it was some sort of strategy to get media attention for a flagging career. This sort of silly speculation hurt, but the new sense Cliff had of God now being in charge of his life overcame any frustrating gossip.

His faith has deepened over the years, and as he looks at all the Christians there are now in the entertainment business, Cliff is glad that he was the first to stand up and be counted.

'Many of us who live a very public life know how easy it is for our perspectives and priorities to get badly distorted from time to time,' he says. 'Insecurities and fears, as well as inflated egos, can all be disruptive and deceptive influences.

'This verse from Philippians, "I have the strength to face

all conditions by the power that God gives me", helps me keep my perspectives in line and is a constant source of encouragement when I have to face all manner of challenges and responsibilities.

'Firstly, it's God who does the enabling, and any success or achievement is thanks to his strength, not mine; and secondly, that strength is always available, so that no task becomes impossible.'

This is Cliff's own prayer:

## Everything Is Possible

Dear Lord,
Remind me that in my strength alone I can achieve little, but that in yours all things are possible. Thank you for that never-failing resource.
Amen.

## I Give You Myself

Lord Jesus,
I give you my hands to do your work.
I give you my feet to go your way.
I give you my eyes to see as you do.
I give you my tongue to speak your words.
I give you my mind that you may think in me.
I give you my spirit that you may pray in me.
Above all,
I give you my heart that you may love in me
your Father and all mankind.
I give you my whole self that you may grow in me,

so that it is you, Lord Jesus,
who live and work and pray in me.

Author unknown

## Margaret Savage

Margaret Savage was born in Glasgow and began her singing career with a Scottish choir. She auditioned for George
Mitchell and it didn't take long for her obvious talent and
ability to sing a wide range of music to be recognized. She
was soon offered the leading role in BBC TV's popular
*Black and White Minstrel Show* followed by two successful three-year runs in the record-breaking stage version at
London's Victoria Palace.

The fantastic success of the Minstrels on radio, records,
stage and television all over the world is almost without
parallel in the history of showbusiness and, without doubt,
Margaret has played a large and important part in contributing to that success.

She has been trying to 'retire' from the business for some
years, but her popularity always ensures producers call her
back, including for a recent four-year revival of the Minstrels
on stage with her fellow co-stars from the BBC TV series.
She still enjoys singing and leading the congregation at her
local church on Sundays.

Margaret says, 'Having juggled a family of four including one with special needs and a career in showbusiness I
have found that a great deal of patience and understanding
is needed, and I pray for the strength to cope with all I am
sent. It's also good to take a few minutes to pay a visit to a
church away from all the hubbub of life's busy traffic.

'I just talk to God as I would to a best friend. I have many favourite prayers, but a simple little prayer that I learned at school, which I often still say morning or night for myself or friends, is the following one.'

## By My Side

Angel of God my guardian dear
To whom God's love commits me here.
Ever this day/night be at my side
To watch and guard to rule and guide. Amen.

## Prayer for Self-Motivation

Omnipotent God, vitality of life,
Your strength supplies my motivation.
I am stirred in the path of your will.
Maintain my self-motivation to always
Search, find, examine, will and act
Upon the truths placed before me.
May I become a driving force for others,
Encouraging them to pick up their crosses
And follow the virtuous road of life.
I thank you for your continued vigour
That coexists in my whole being,
My soul, my spirit and my body!
Amen.

Author unknown

# David Suchet

David Suchet plays one of the most famous detectives in the world, and walking through a door is not as easy as it seems when you are the quick-stepping Belgian Hercule Poirot. Everything is planned meticulously, and the padding David wears for his part is hot and stuffy, but he is known for many other superb roles on stage, film and television.

'I'm a character actor who seems to play strange, idiosyncratic people who are outsiders or loners,' he explains. 'Being well known gives me the opportunity to play some wonderfully interesting roles, all different. I like that. It confuses people.'

But his roles were not always chosen by himself. At one point David would allow tarot cards to pick the next job for him: 'For some time I had been into Zen Buddhism, yoga, tarot, astrology and spiritism, always searching for something, but never finding it.'

On a trip to America to appear in a new Spielberg film, he had a sudden urge to read the Bible. Switching on the television in his room he was amazed to find it advertise the Bible. He then went to his bedside drawer, remembering the Gideon Bibles often placed there, only to find it empty. Feeling 'terribly embarrassed' he went out to buy a copy of the New Testament, and returning to his room went to put it in his bedside drawer. There, to his amazement, lay a Gideon Bible.

'I opened it and started to read from Acts to Paul's letters, Romans and Corinthians. It was only after that I came to the Gospels. I suddenly discovered the way that life should be followed, and I remember thinking, "Goodness me, here it is all this time, and I never saw it in the very thing that I had discarded at school as a lot of history for exams."'

Interestingly, David was playing the part of a psychopathic killer at the time!

'Reading the Bible,' he says, 'was more than just an intellectual exercise; it was a fascinating journey. I thought that if I could be like this, even a little bit each day, then I would have a goal for life.'

Over the next few months his spiritual journey worked through many boundaries of doubt and the need for answers, and he describes his walk as '. . . a very lonely and tortuous path, but I was confident that this was the path on which God was taking me. I've learned a great deal about putting my trust in an invisible God, trusting that which is unseen.'

Another problem is being used by others, particularly when you feel you ought to say 'yes' to other Christians. For example, David was leaving a Christian recording studio one day, when he was suddenly placed in front of a large poster and had photos taken to advertise a product. Pressure has often been placed on him to speak at Christian events too, without him being ready to give in this way. It's sad when the Church sees people in the business as public property.

The roles David now plays are influenced by his Christian faith. He prays about which parts he accepts, but it's important for any actor to stay in the real world. 'The world of drama and entertainment is full of characters and situations that can hardly be called "Christian". It would be very easy to fall into the temptation to turn round and say I was unable to play murderers now,' he says.

'As an actor I have to remain open to portray any type of character, even the unpleasant ones. As Christians, we are called to be lights in the darkness and if by playing an unsavoury part in a film I can show the destruction that evil can bring into our lives, I feel I am being that light.

'Solving the mystery of life has changed me in many ways, and I'm thrilled that I can enjoy a new and deep relationship with the one who made me, loves me, and will guide me every step of the way.'

David has asked to adopt the Christians in Entertainment prayer for Entertainment Sunday:

## The Christians in Entertainment Prayer

We praise you and thank you that you are the giver of all that is good and worthwhile and that you have created gifts of entertainment to be used in your world. We ask that you will inspire and encourage all who work in theatres, television and radio.

We pray for all those working in the entertainment business, including actors as they bring drama to life, comedians as they remind us how to laugh, dancers as they provide elegance and beauty and singers as they offer the wonder of music.

We pay that all entertainment will be used as a tool for understanding, healing, relaxation, enriching and to express your love for humanity. Amen.

A woman invited some people to dinner. At the table, she turned to her six-year-old daughter and said, 'Would you like to say grace?'

'I wouldn't know what to say,' the little girl replied.

'Just say what you heard Mummy say earlier,' the mother said.

The little girl bowed her head and said, 'Dear Lord, why on earth did I invite all these people to dinner?'

## Tim Vine

Tim Vine was recently hailed by the *Guardian* newspaper as 'continuously funny and utterly unique'.

Hailed as one of the UK's best new comedians, Tim is seen almost everywhere from his new BBC sitcom *Not Going Out* to celebrity chat shows, panel games, and even being the winner of *Celebrity Mastermind*.

Tim is one of those rare comedians who always uses clean material. 'I don't actually sit down and think I mustn't swear because I'm a Christian; it just wouldn't fit into my style of act.'

Comedy is at the heart of all that he does and even a visit to his website offers a laugh a minute:

'I was reading a book . . . "the history of glue" . . . I couldn't put it down.'

'Now, most dentists' chairs go up and down, don't they? The one I was in went back and forwards. I thought, "This is unusual." And the dentist said to me, "Mr Vine, get out of the filing cabinet." '

'So I got home, and the phone was ringing. I picked it up, and said, "Who's speaking, please?" And a voice said "You are." '

'So I rang up a local building firm. I said, "I want a skip outside my house." He said, "I'm not stopping you." '

'You know, somebody actually complimented me on my driving today. They left a little note on the windscreen; it said "Parking Fine". So that was nice.'

Tim says that God created the gift of humour, and is grateful he gets so many chances to share it.

'This is a dressing-room prayer I wrote when nervously waiting to go out on stage,' Tim explains. 'It's one that I often repeat in my mind in the middle of my act and reminds me that although in life things don't always go to plan, God is still there beside us every step of the way and will help us re-focus when we get sidetracked . . .'

## Waiting in the Wings

Dear Lord,

Help me to make your great gift of laughter resound in this room tonight, and, Lord, if everyone is laughing except for one man help me not to be distracted by his grumpy face.

Help me to concentrate on the hundreds of people who are laughing and not this one man who, for some reason, doesn't like any of my jokes.

Lord, help me not to be mildly irritated that he came to see me at all when clearly he doesn't like me, but most of all, Lord, thank you for laughter and how it raises the spirits of the lonely and heals the aching bones.

Lord, what's wrong with that bloke and why is he not even smiling?

Lord, why do I keep staring at him? Please stop me staring at him. Amen.

# Tony Vino

Tony Vino has been touring the comedy scene since early 2005. A finalist in the 2006 'Funny Bones' competition, Tony has enjoyed recognition as a comedian and, notably, comedy compère of renown.

He is best known for the way he seamlessly mixes well-thought-out observational humour with audience interaction and quick-witted responses. His life and interests are wide ranging, and so is his material, all performed in a warm, friendly and non-offensive style.

Tony heads up the comedy at the Greenbelt Festival and is the resident compère of Just Fair Laughs, a Fair Trade comedy agency that runs several weekly and monthly comedy nights in pubs and theatres across the UK.

Well aware of social and political issues, Tony has been called upon to entertain at many high-profile events for charities such as Christian Aid, Oxfam, Fairtrade Foundation and TearFund. He does warm-up work for BBC *Songs of Praise*. When hosting festivals and corporate events, his confident, effervescent persona has been found ideal for engaging crowds in their hundreds and thousands.

His faith informs all of his on-stage style and content as Tony believes passionately in comedy that is uplifting and life-affirming.

'My faith informs my performances,' he explains, 'but I'm determined not to let my stand-up turn preachy. Within the comedy scene, it can be a challenge to create cutting-edge comedy when you don't swear or use offensive material. I always have at the back of my mind that my comedy should be life-affirming and joy-bringing. It's less a case of what jokes I won't do, but more what I am pitching towards.'

# In Time of Debt

Almighty, everlasting God,
we beg of you to help us soon to pay off our debts to our
    fellow men.
Give us strength and courage to persevere until the last
    penny is paid.
Give patience to those to whom we are in debt,
and let them not treat us unjustly.
Help us have great confidence in you and in the
    workings of your providence,
trusting that you will always direct things to our
    greatest good.

Make us also fully realize that no debt to our fellow men
can begin to equal the debt that we owe you on account
    of our sins,
to say nothing of the immense debt we owe you
for the gifts of your divine grace.
These we could never pay at all but for the coming of
    your Son,
our Lord, Jesus Christ.
To him be all honour and thanksgiving, now and
    forever. Amen.

Author unknown

# Rick Wakeman

Rick Wakeman is known to millions for his amazing keyboard skills and brilliant compositions.

He has enjoyed a career spanning several decades, from his earliest days as a concert pianist through to his phenomenally successful solo albums such as *Journey to the Centre of the Earth* and *The Six Wives of Henry the Eighth*. Other classic albums with his group Yes include *Fragile*, *Close to the Edge* and, on his own, *The New Gospels*, which musically traced the life of Jesus, and the myths and legends of King Arthur.

Rick is well known for his love of golf and his outrageous sense of humour, yet his life has not been laughter all the way. Three marriages, a heart attack at 25, and a long struggle with stardom have all taken their toll, but it was his discovery of God that was to change his life.

'Despite being baptized at 19, I pushed God further and further away, as my love of music became more and more important,' explains Rick. It wasn't until he met model Nina Carter that the hunt to find a church that would marry them started to draw them closer to a God they had both abandoned many years before. Overjoyed at being accepted by a church that received them in true Christian love, 'I was given a renewed faith in the Church that had been lacking for more than 15 years,' recalls Rick.

The journey back to God had begun. One night while on tour in Sydney, Australia, struggling with an alcoholic problem, Rick sat on his bed and cried. 'I had never felt so low in my entire life,' he recalls, 'and I realized I had never really been in control of my life, although I thought I was.' Explaining how a strange calmness came over the room, he knew there was only one thing left to do. 'The decision was to put my life back into God's hands. I asked him then and there to forgive me for all that I had done and to give me the strength to start again.' Rick knew he was back in safe hands. As if confirming this, Rick received a BAFTA award in 1997 for his services to the industry.

'In simple terms, I don't know how to fly a plane and don't particularly want to,' Rick explains. 'However, I have every faith in the pilot and put my trust in him to get me safely to my destination. I also don't have even a millionth of God's understanding and knowledge of this world he created, or what his destiny is for us all. However, I have every faith in him as my pilot, and put my trust in him to get me to my destination along the route he has chosen for me.'

## Trusting You

Dear Lord, help us to understand the limitations of our understanding. Help us to accept that in this world there are many questions which will remain unanswered. Give us peace of mind to know that you are in total control and that you alone know the purpose of everything that happens to us, both as individuals and also as part of an ever-changing and confusing world.

Teach me not to query that which you and you alone have control over. Help us to accept that you have a reason for everything that happens to us and others, however unacceptable it may appear at the time.

We need to give you our trust completely, Lord, which is not always easy to do. It is hard sometimes for us to differentiate between attacks from the Devil and tests that you send from above.

With your strength, your guidance and the knowledge of your supreme understanding, we can perhaps begin to fulfil the purpose for which you placed us on this earth. Without you, we would never understand. Amen.

**St Genesius**, the patron saint of actors, was a popular actor in Roman times. He had a pretty good gig, doing shows for the emperor, commercials for wine makers, and stuff like that.

Then he was forced by the emperor to do a blasphemous play, written by – the emperor. Like all actors, he took the gig, even though it wasn't his cup of tea. Then, in the middle of the show, he suddenly got a conscience. He stopped the show, complained about the script, and embraced Christianity.

For this act of ad-libbing, he was drawn and quartered, beheaded, and chopped into little pieces. Not in that order. This made him the first artist to lose a government arts grant.

## Tabitha Webb

Tabitha Webb almost popped out of the womb singing. She started out as a choral scholar at 16, winning the BBC Choir-girl of the Year competition, thrusting her into the world of professionals with national television, radio and recording experience that kick-started a rather obvious career choice to all who knew this little girl with the soaring voice!

Just scraping 5 feet with size two feet, you might think she could make a career playing fairies, children, angels, etc. – and, yes, as she started off as an opera singer, these parts featured a lot! She has sung as soloist in venues such as the Royal Albert Hall, Royal Opera House, Cardiff International Arena, Cheltenham and Buxton festivals to name a few.

Although she greatly enjoyed the concert stage and oratorio work, it is 'the smell of the greasepaint, the roar of the crowd' that always drew her to theatrical stage work.

The last few years have seen her in *The Phantom of the Opera*, understudying the part of Christine, and she is currently in *Les Misérables*, understudying Cosette. Juggling the demands of eight tiring shows a week, two days teaching singing in a private school in Kent, keeping up with the mortgage, and trying to be a good wife to her adorable, patient husband Robbie, a musician, has its challenges! But with an amazingly supportive Medway Family Church and a heavenly Father who knows her better than she knows herself, she's keeping her head firmly above water. They live happily in their tiny house in Rochester with an overly loving rescue-cat called Bashment.

'God put us Christians in every walk of life to be "salt and light" wherever we are, even in the theatre. I always want to pray that I do a good job of it, of course, but it doesn't always happen as we would like it to. Knowing such grace that God has over our failings and yet knowing he delights in our tiny steps of obedience towards him is so encouraging.

'As a very little girl I listened and sang along to Keith Green songs a lot. Wow, could that man put across a song from the heart! Many of them are prayers, and this one has meant so much to me growing up as a Christian. It's a big prayer to pray, but I just have to offer myself and he'll take care of the rest. I still can't sing it without welling up, and I pray this now as I did when I was ten . . .'

TABITHA WEBB

## Make My Life a Prayer

Make my life a prayer to you.
I want to do what you want me to.
No empty words and no white lies,
No token prayers, no compromise.

I want to shine the light you gave
Through your Son, you sent to save us
From ourselves and our despair.
It comforts me to know you're really there.

Well I want to thank you now
For being patient with me.
Oh it's so hard to see
When my eyes are on me.
I guess I'll have to trust
And just believe what you say.
Oh you're coming again,
Coming to take me away.

I want to die and let you give
Your life to me, so I might live
And share the hope you gave to me,
The love that set me free!

I want to tell the world out there
You're not some fable or fairy tale
That I've made up inside my head.
You're God, the Son, you've risen from the dead!

Well I want to thank you now
For being patient with me.
Oh it's so hard to see
When my eyes are on me.
I guess I'll have to trust

117

And just believe what you say.
Oh you're coming again,
Coming to take me away!

I want to die and let you give
Your life to me, so I might live
And share the hope you gave to me.
I want to share the love that set me free!

Keith Green

## Knowing Me Better

I thank you, Lord,
for knowing me better than I know myself,
and for letting me know myself
better than others know me.
Make me, I pray you,
better than they suppose,
and forgive me for what they do not know.

Author unknown

## Frank Williams

Frank Williams is one of the best-known faces in the most popular classic comedy BBC TV series of all time, *Dad's Army*. Yet the 'vicar' in real life has a strong Christian faith and a lifelong commitment to the Church. Even after 20 years, *Dad's Army* continues to regularly pull in millions of viewers for each repeated episode. Video, audio tapes,

DVDs and books about the series remain bestsellers, and successfully bridge the generation gap like no other.

The originators of the series, David Croft and Jimmy Perry, chose Frank Williams to create the role of the wonderfully eccentric vicar who was always slightly tetchy as he tried to come to terms with the elderly platoon's invasion of his beloved church hall. Frank was perfectly cast in *Dad's Army* and enjoyed its long run.

However, Frank has spent a lifetime in the world of entertainment and appeared in many other highly successful productions including Granada TV's *The Army Game* and as the bishop in the BBC's *You Rang, M'Lord?* Appearances in plays, pantomimes, and over 30 films have seen him work with some of the world's leading stars. Several of his own plays have been produced to date.

Despite his instant recognition in public, he remains a very private man, and his Christian faith is his bedrock. Frank tells the story of his life in his autobiography, *Vicar to Dad's Army*, and often accepts invitations to churches around the UK to talk about his life, work and faith.

'When I watch television these days,' Frank says, 'I do sometimes wonder what's happened to our ideas about humour. Of course, there has always been in England a great tradition of anarchic, disrespectful bawdy humour from Chaucer onwards, but in the past it had some style, some wit, and some purpose. Now all too often what we get is the kind of sniggering smut that I might have thought funny when I was still at my prep school.

'We need to understand that television does not only reflect life, but it is a powerful medium which also has a strong influence in actually forming the culture in which we live.

'So what do I want from television? I want the comedy to be witty and amusing with good characters and funny situations. I want the drama to entertain but I also want it to stimulate my mind and make me think about the problems that people face. I want it to help me to understand situations that I will probably never experience for myself. I want it to help me to be compassionate. I want it to help me laugh, and I want it to make me weep. I want it to be responsible and have ideals. At its best it should enrich the spirit and deepen our understanding of what it means to be a human being made in the image of God.

'I suppose for me, the prayer of the Actors' Church Union says it all.'

### Actors' Church Union Prayer

Oh God, the King of Glory, who in the making of man didst bestow upon him the gift of tears and the sense of joy, and didst implant in his nature, the need for recreation of mind and body; give to those who minister to that need through drama and music in the calling of the theatrical profession, a high ideal, a pure intention and the sense of great responsibility. And both to them and to those who accept their ministry give the will so to use it that it may be for the enrichment of human character and for thy greater glory. Amen.

### Can We Really Believe God Loves Us?

Our Father.
You have invited us to pray about everything.
The fact that we haven't always done so is no reflection on your greatness or your love.
We just have a hard time believing you could love nobodies and failures like us.

The cross of Jesus says otherwise, doesn't it?
Says it loud and clear.
Since you love us fiercely and desire only to bless us,
would you forgive us for all the sorry prayers we have
sent your way and which are clogging heaven's golden
gutters?
Help us to believe in your goodness and your grace
and your willingness to bless us. May we begin today
praying seriously about the things and the people who
matter most to us.
Through Jesus our Lord. Amen.

Joe McKeever

## And it's goodbye from me . . .

I could hardly ask all my showbiz friends to contribute
their personal or adopted prayers without offering a
prayer of my own, could I . . . ?

# Chris Gidney

Chris Gidney comes from a showbusiness family, and at
the age of nine formed a comedy magic double-act with
his father. Since then he has spent a lifetime in the profession as entertainer, producer, director and author, working
with numerous artistes from the legendary Frank Sinatra to
Sir Cliff Richard. Joining London's West End in 1980, he
enjoyed 12 consecutive productions before moving to BBC
Television, working on such classic programmes as *Blue
Peter*, and *That's Life* with Esther Rantzen.

Based on his extensive friendships within the profession, his first book, *In the Limelight*, was published in 1993 and since then he has authored more than 28 books covering various aspects of life in showbusiness. He has also written for BBC Radio and a number of newspapers and periodicals.

As a freelance director and producer, he is responsible for a number of unique stage, television and radio productions, while his recording company Fusion has produced several music, audio and video releases. In 2004 he co-founded That's Entertainment Productions (TEP), which specializes in bringing high-quality family entertainment with integrity to the commercial theatre. TEP produces summer seasons for popular resorts such as Blackpool, Bournemouth and Eastbourne, and has several productions on the road at any one time.

Chris formed the showbusiness charity Christians in Entertainment in 1982, which continues to provide backstage support for professionals in the entertainment industry, and he remains the director of this organization.

'So, here is my prayer . . . written by me at two o'clock in the morning. That's normal for me. I often find myself writing paragraphs, directing shows, or coming up with creative ideas at the most unusual of times. Showbiz is a topsy-turvy world at the best of times. We go to work when everyone else is coming home, go to bed when everyone else is getting up, eat breakfast when everyone else is having lunch, and work hardest when everyone else is on holiday. Whichever way you look at it, life is still a wonderful gift, and my prayer tries to reflect this.'

## The Gift

Thank you, Lord,
For skills and gifts you gave without measure,
For art and theatre and films to treasure.

For laughing with me at the funniness of life,
Your guidance and support through trouble and strife.

Your care and love shown all along the way,
The friends you sent to cheer me on each day.

The total forgiveness you always show
When all I cause is sorrow and woe.

The patient way you stand and wait
While those mistakes I constantly make.

For parents past and family now,
For children who can show me how.

The way you love me despite myself
And never leave me on the shelf.

A future hope that you promised me,
A life that will end in eternity.

Thank you, Lord.

# Entertainment Sunday

The entertainment business may seem full of glitz and glamour, but it can be one of the loneliest, most insecure and isolated places in which to work. Every year Christians in Entertainment offers churches and individuals across the UK the opportunity to spare a thought and a prayer for those working in front of the footlights, microphone and camera. Churches are given a free DVD with backstage glimpses of the charity's work, never seen before.

Entertainment is a service industry, but because of its very nature it's easy to forget that those who work in it are often under a huge amount of pressure whether it be unemployment, separation from their families, or the stress of keeping a career alive in a fast-moving industry.

Christians in Entertainment (CIE) supports those in the profession from all levels of belief who are working away from family, friends and perhaps church. Through our backstage groups, dressing-room Bibles, one-to-one visits and our prayer textline, CIE offers opportunities for performers at every level of the profession to explore what the Christian faith might mean to them.

# Acknowledgements

My thanks go to all who have contributed to this book. Authors of the prayers have been credited where known, but if we have omitted to credit any inclusions, or our efforts to contact copyright owners of any material used has not been successful, please let us know and full acknowledgement will be made in any future additions.

Thanks to Sally Goring, my pastoral assistant at Christians in Entertainment, who is the best listener and pray-er I have ever met.

I am very grateful to Charles Case, my mate who sat in his shed day after day drawing the hilarious and often poignant illustrations for this book, and to Ruth Oliver for her help and hilarious discussions covering many and varied interesting topics relating to church and faith.

# Websites

Many of those entertainers who have kindly contributed to this book have their own websites full of funny stories, pictures and the occasional prayer or two!

I have listed as many as possible below:

| | |
|---|---|
| John Archer – magician | www.john-archer.com |
| Cannon & Ball – comedy double act | www.cannonandball.co.uk |
| John Byrne – entertainment journalist | www.showbusiness-success.com |
| Jason Carter – singer | www.jasoncarter.net |
| Charlie Case – clown and entertainer | www.charliecase.biz |
| Jimmy Cricket – comedian | www.jimmycricket.co.uk |
| Steve Fortune – actor | www.stevefortune.com |
| George Hamilton IV – singer | www. georgeiv.net |
| Jesse Joyner – juggler | www.JesseTheJuggler.com |
| Shekhar Kapur – film director | www.shekharkapur.com |
| Janey Lee Grace – presenter | www.imperfectlynatural.com |
| Steve Legg – escapologist | www.stevelegg.com |
| Syd Little – comedian | www.shorehillarts.co.uk |
| Danny Owen – singer | www.dannyowen.co.uk |
| James Owen – entertainer | www.jamesowen.biz |

| | |
|---|---|
| Nick Page – broadcaster and producer | www.shorehillarts.co.uk |
| Lance Pierson – actor | www.lancepierson.org |
| Sir Cliff Richard – singer | www.cliffrichard.org |
| Tim Vine – comedian | www.timvine.com |
| Tony Vino – comedian | www.tonyvino.co.uk |

## Useful Resources

To book a celebrity guest for your event: www.shorehillarts.co.uk

Christians in Entertainment: www.cieweb.org.uk

Christian Prayers Resource: www.prayer-and-prayers.info

Christian Jugglers' Association: www.christianjuggling.com

Prayers and other inspirations: www.joemckeever.com

The Son Newspaper: www.theson.org.uk

# Index of Prayers

## INDEX OF PRAYERS